Aēsop.
and
the PARIS REVIEW

A partnership extended

It is our pleasure to partner with *The Paris Review*
in offering this esteemed quarterly for purchase at
select Aesop spaces around the globe.

You will find each new edition of *The Paris Review*
at thirty Aesop doors globally, including signature stores in
Tiquetonne, Paris; Mitte, Berlin; and Prinsensgate, Oslo.
It is also available at Aesop Online in Australia, France,
Hong Kong, Japan and the UK.

Discover more about this literary partnership
at aesop.com

20th CENTURY BOY

Duncan Hannah

"BY TURNS ROMANTIC, EROTIC, DRAMATIC, AND HILARIOUS...A portrait of a young artist truly coming of age." —*Kirkus Reviews*

"IMMERSES THE READER IN A HISTORY OF BEAUTY from the Nouvelle vague to meetings with David Hockney." —Thurston Moore, co-founder of Sonic Youth

"*What would I change? A futile question. It is what it is. No regrets.*"

"**THIS IS NOT A MEMOIR.** THESE ARE JOURNALS, BEGUN IN 1970, AT THE AGE OF SEVENTEEN, WRITTEN AS IT HAPPENED, FILLED WITH YOUTHFUL INDISCRETIONS. IT'S ALL TRUE."

Knopf

the PARIS

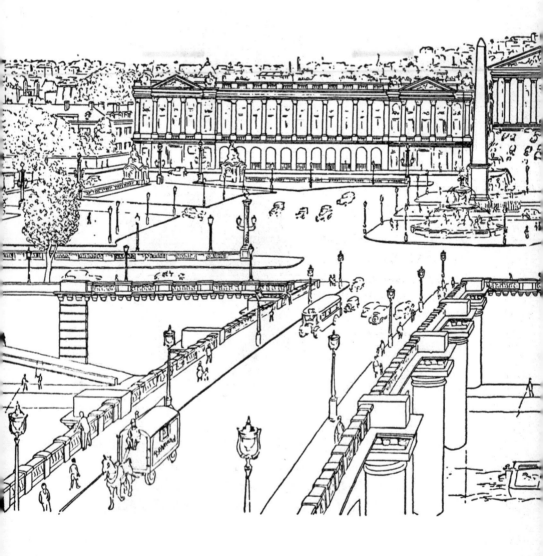

REVIEW

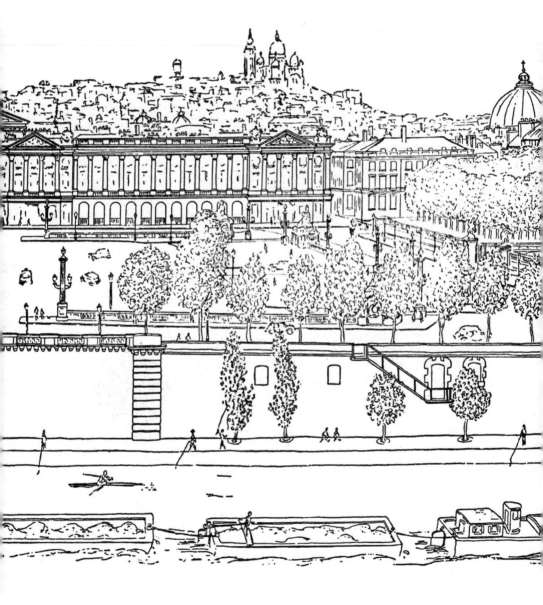

544 WEST 27th STREET *new york, new york 10001*

GABR

HEA

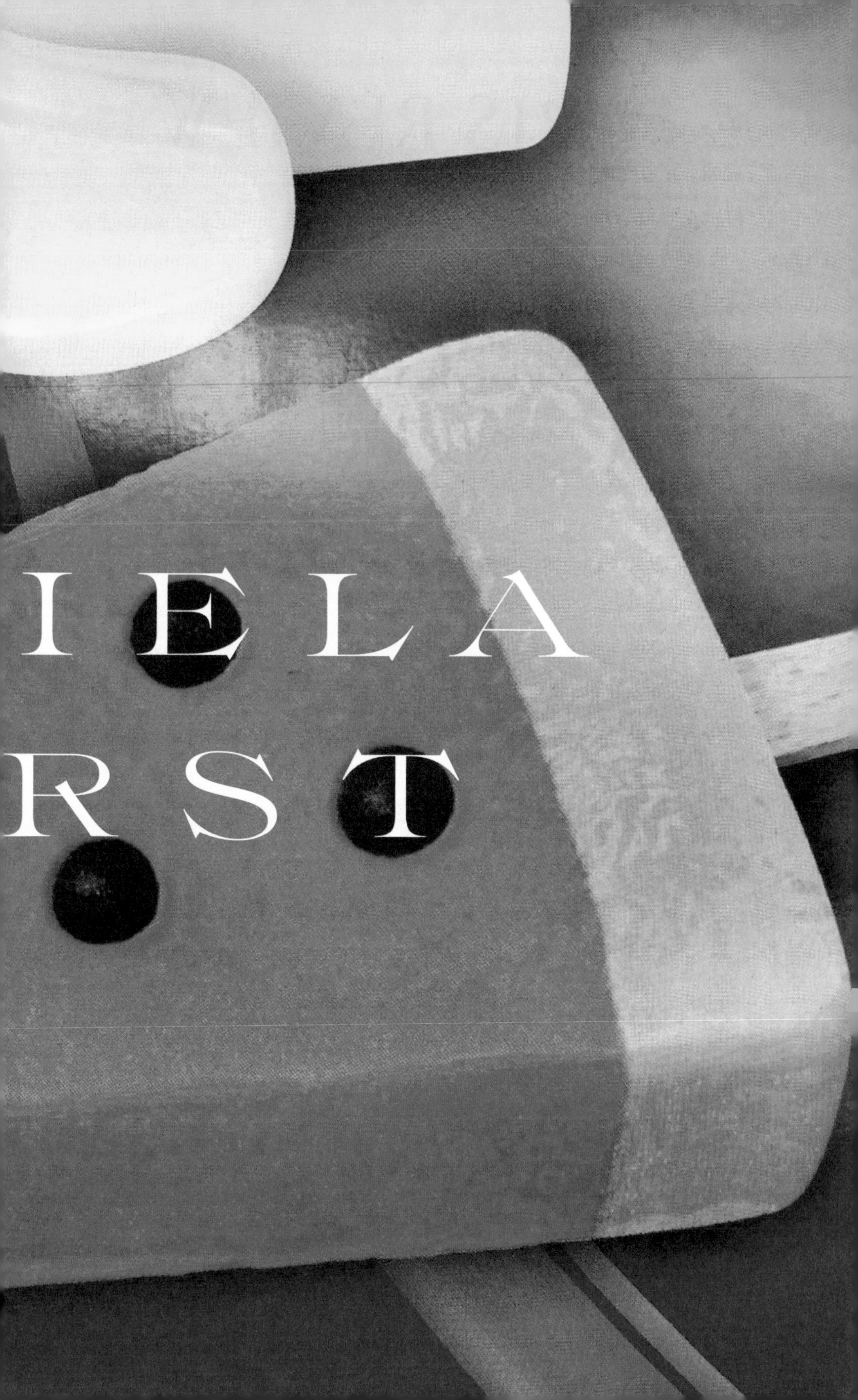
IELA
RST

the PARIS REVIEW

GEORGE PLIMPTON 1927–2003

The Paris Review (issn #0031–2037) is published quarterly by The Paris Review Foundation, Inc. at 544 West 27th Street, New York, NY 10001. Vol. 60, No. 224, Spring 2018. Terry McDonell, President; William B. Beekman, Secretary; Lawrence H. Guffey, Treasurer. Please give six weeks notice of change of address. Periodicals postage paid at New York, NY, and at additional mailing offices. Postmaster: please send address changes to The Paris Review, PO Box 8524, Big Sandy, TX 75755-8524. For subscriptions, please call toll-free: (866) 354-0212. From outside the U.S.: (903) 636-1118. • While The Paris Review welcomes the submission of unsolicited manuscripts, it cannot accept responsibility for their loss or engage in related correspondence. Please send manuscripts with a self-addressed, stamped envelope to The Paris Review, 544 West 27th Street, New York, NY 10001. For additional information, please visit www.theparisreview.org. Printed in the United States. Copyright © 2018 by The Paris Review Foundation, Inc.

KOREAN
LITERATURE
NOW

Quarterly magazine on
Korean literature and translation

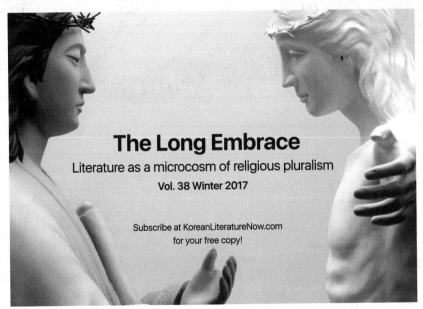

The Long Embrace
Literature as a microcosm of religious pluralism
Vol. 38 Winter 2017

Subscribe at KoreanLiteratureNow.com
for your free copy!

NUMBER 224

Cover: Etel Adnan. Frontispiece: William Pène du Bois, Paris View.

TUESDAY
APRIL 3, 2018
the PARIS REVIEW
SPRING REVEL

HONORING
JOY WILLIAMS

BENEFIT CHAIR JOHN WATERS

FOR TICKET AND ADDITIONAL INFORMATION
PLEASE CONTACT JULIA BERICK
(212) 343-1333 REVEL@THEPARISREVIEW.ORG

WWW.THEPARISREVIEW.ORG

DESIGN BY STRICK & WILLIAMS

Flour

—

JOY WILLIAMS

T he driver and I got a late start. I usually decide on these excursions the night before, but it was late in the morning when I informed the friend who was coming to visit me for the weekend that I had to cancel, it was absolutely necessary for me to cancel. I had got it in my head that in her presence some calamity or another would arise and she would have to assist me in some way, rush me to a physician or something. She would be grateful she was there for me perhaps, but I would find it a terrific annoyance and embarrassment. I gave some other excuse for the disinvitation of course. Pipes. I think it was broken pipes. I should have written it down so I don't use it again.

I cleaned the house, which was very much in need of cleaning, for I had been putting it off. Still, my commitment was not great and I neglected the windows as usual. The dogs had pressed against them day and night for years. Their breaths are etched in the glass now, very lightly etched.

By departing so late, we could not make our customary first stop. The driver and I usually spend two nights in lodgings on our route. This time three nights would be necessary. We take separate rooms, of course. If by chance we should come across one another in the restaurant or the hallways, we offer no acknowledgment.

The car is a big one, encompassing three rows, three tiers behind the driver. It amuses me to think of them as the celestial, the terrestrial, and the chthonic. In fact, I quite believe that all things—every moment, every vision, every departure and arrival—possess the celestial, the terrestrial, and the chthonic.

The dogs had pretty much stayed in the terrestrial section where their beds were, as well as a few empty plastic bottles. They liked to play with them, make them crackle and clatter. Sometimes I ride in the chthonic with the luggage, the boots and coats, the boxes of fruit and gin and books. It smells strangely good back there, coolly hopeful and warmly worn at once. But usually I stretch out in the seat behind the driver and watch the landscape change as we rise from the desert floor.

Shockingly, it is almost two o'clock in the afternoon. We will not get far today!

When the driver and I first met—when I was interviewing him, you might say—he told me that he was studying Coptic.

Naturally, I did not believe this for one moment.

Without any encouragement from me he said, "The verb forms and tenses of Coptic are interesting. For example, some tenses that we English speakers do not have are the circumstantial, the habitual, the third future, the fourth future, the optative, and tenses of unfulfilled action signifying *until* and *not yet*. I am working now on translating and interpreting the story about the woman carrying flour to her home in a jar that is broken."

"The flour all pours out?" I said.

"Why yes." He seemed pleased.

Everyone knows the story of the woman and the flour. Who did he think he was kidding? Still, you're never drawn to a person for the reasons you think. Besides, he was the only one who applied for the position I sought, which I had kept purposefully vague, and parsing every nuance of the woman and the jar would keep him occupied at least.

We are at a crossroads light behind a new, bright yellow truck. When the light changes and the truck accelerates, a dense cloud of black smoke erupts from the tailpipe. People spend more than a thousand dollars to customize their vehicles for this effect, which honors freedom and individuality. It takes a moment for the simple clarity of the air and sky to reassert itself.

When a little baby dies you think, If they can do it with such wonderment, so can I.

The bright yellow truck, the yolk-colored truck, dances away. He is not going in our direction, though perhaps he quite is, and our driver is graciously finding a detour for my sake. Rather than discussing the wisdom of this—will we find a decent place to stay when dusk descends—I leave my perch and crawl over the backs of seats to the very rear, the cozy chthonic. There is scarcely room for me to curl, to burrow, and surprisingly I do not even feel comfortable here.

Dusk is not nearly as considerate as is generally assumed. One thinks it offers a reasonable amount of time to adjust to night descendant, but the reality is it does not. With only moments to spare, we sweep under the portico of a large hotel that has seen better days.

The driver goes in to address the desk while I pick about among the rubble in the back. Sometimes I like to bring my own lamp into these places, but I feel too tired to locate the cord, then follow the cord. I am remarkably tired. I look instead at the gardens that rim the crescent of the drive. Though they are not extensive, someone cares for them, really cares. I feel better watching them, as though I have just enjoyed a cocktail, though that is still ahead of me, thank God.

(In the morning the gardens would not seem nearly as responsibly cared for, but I was paying less attention to them then.)

The driver has arranged for everything. He escorts me to an adequate room, smiles as guilelessly as the boy he so seems to be, and says good night. Later I go down for my cocktails in the cavernous dining room made tragic with the heads of animals and loud with the happy screams of tourists. There are commendable ruins nearby, apparently. We would never have stopped here had I been more decisive earlier.

We leave at daybreak, the reasoning being that we would make up some time. Preposterous of course. One cannot make up time. One can make up a story or a face or a bed. Ugh. I find it all repellent. My bed, by the way, was so uncomfortable. I would not have been surprised if, on tearing the mattress open, I'd have found it to be stuffed with rocks. The driver says apologetically that he had spent a restful night, though he had slept little, as he was working on his translation.

"The art of translation is very forgiving, isn't it," I say.

"Forgiving?" he repeats.

For a while I ride up front with him but find I can gain no perspective. We are climbing, climbing, there are switchbacks and signs of warning in the bright falsity of daylight, and nature pressing in around us, fierce yet helpless, regarding us with distaste.

I think of my friend. She might not have received the message and could be knocking at the door of my house this very moment. She might have even already left once and returned. But I cannot think about her for long. We both have betrayed one another more than once.

AFTER A FEW HOURS, though we had not made up one minute of lost time, the driver asks if I would like to stop for a moment. He pulls off the road and spreads the blanket—which we have used often for this purpose—upon the ground and puts out bread and water. I had once tried to make the bread myself, but it was dreadful. I don't know where it's acquired now. We seldom eat much of it. We never finish it. Sometimes we don't even begin, though I don't wish to think we waste it. The sun is warm, the air feels fresh and good, but I feel that the small pleasure I am taking in this instant is significant only to the extent that it can be remembered, and once again I am compelled to be dissatisfied.

The car looms beside us, handsome, without agency. The driver had once confessed to me that he loved it as he had loved nothing in his life before and that if I ever found it necessary to separate him from its care he would probably kill himself.

He is such a child, I thought at the time, but I did not reassure him. I might even have smiled, possibly laughed, his question was so naive. Of course, the both of them could crush me like an insect at any time. It is a serious business, a most serious business.

He packs up the bread and water and folds up the blanket, the raveling border of which I pretend not to notice. What he should be doing in the evening is repairing our picnic blanket, or at the very least determining how it can be displayed without calling attention to its degradation. Instead, he spends the nights searching for the missing word in some Coptic riddle. Or so he claims.

Hours pass rather senselessly, as they often do. I do some thinking once again in the rear, in my cannily constructed chthonic, but nothing of any real import. When we stop again, dusk is just beginning to assemble her portentous armies. The lodging is once again unfamiliar. It might have been plucked out of a hat, as they say. Again it is a hotel from an earlier time, restored to partial grandeur. There seems to be a niche of Texas billionaires who specialize in these labors of love. What is their fantasy really, I wonder. With very little inquiry I learn that one of the new owners is an artist. Her paintings are everywhere, her specialty scenes of dinner parties where the well-known dead are guests. Frida Kahlo and her parrots are there, for example. I think they are parrots.

In my room is a fruit basket, which contains a single orange. Quite naturally, I am afraid to eat it. The room is pleasant enough, but there is a certain beyondness to it. I cannot explain this at all but I very much want to discuss it with the driver. Yet when I come upon him later, drinking a glass of wine on one of the verandas, I ignore him as usual.

Trains rumble past the hotel all night but there are no passengers on them. They carry freight, interminable freight.

The next morning is bitterly cold. I approach breakfast wearing everything I own and even a robe I do not, a fat white thing that is one of the amenities of the hotel. A small fire is burning in the vast fieldstone fireplace. It looks absurd—a few sticks when it could have been mighty logs. There is certainly enough timber surrounding the place.

The driver is seated some distance from the inadequate fire. He is not one for pretending that things offer what they cannot. He, too, is wearing the provided robe, and the sight of it over his dark suit—for it looks as foolish as the fire—prompts me to acknowledge him with a shy wave. I approach him, even sit down opposite him. His notebook is open and he is pressing a pencil against the page. This I have witnessed before.

"Not still the woman with the jar," I tease. "Surely you must be on to another narrative by now."

"I've rendered the road as a distant road," he says.

"But that is nowhere near the end," I protested. "Practically nothing can be known at that point."

"What is important is the quality of the emptiness she eventually discovers," he agrees. "And that is what is so difficult to suggest."

We do not return to our respective rooms but place the robes in a barrel that we believe to be for that purpose.

In the car, the driver says, "I think with a little effort it's very possible we can recover the schedule."

"Excellent," I say.

And we do arrive, though it struck me then as being utterly foreign. But the driver, breaking our comfortable silence at last, says that to him it appeared much the same as always.

Ishion Hutchinson

A HORACE TO HORACE

1

Lost causes confound. Where are you, cousin,
since you swung upside down the iron gate
outside school? The earth is your sky—correct
me, *was*. I blame the missionaries. I blame
myself for getting the words below Annie Vallotton's
fluent drawings. You drew blank. Swung and swung.
The hinges, gnashing in my ears, wing out
her "maximum expression with a minimum
of lines." Impossible, but wait awhile.

2

Me? Undermine the upper classes? What
upper classes, exactly? Copper isn't gold,
nor is there a meadow or a brook
in those crannies wedged on hillside plots—
schemes, excuse me—cinder blocks and grilles
artillery-teetered like upholstered derelicts
amid fruit trees. They, too, are survivors.
They live off the blood franchise I refuse,
with undue respect, to forgive and move on.

3

Even the best possible outcome, you flew
an avenging angel's speed, was possible—
forgive me, *is*. Ivory shade burns your
steep descent up the shortcut bearing
our trampled anonymity,

over frugal marigolds and devil's horsewhips.
When progress takes hold, in whatever form,
it will be belated and advance nothing.
I insist you stride on air. Fierce, tender.

Practicing

CHIA-CHIA LIN

This would have been her favorite season in the Allegheny woods. The shadows of the trees were rickety, and the wind had sap in its scent. But last week, Ty had left; now one day decayed into the next. Their house was abandoned. Only their father, sitting in the dark.

Lumi was building a tepee. She leaned branches against the trunk of a white ash, leaving a triangular opening through which she could crawl in and out. But every time she passed through, a few sticks fell off.

While she was inside the tepee trying to stabilize it, a man's voice said, "This wouldn't do in any situation." From between the weave of sticks, she saw a massive pair of hiking boots and gray corduroy hems.

Once in a while, boys from her bus route rode their dirt bikes across a corner of the property. Ty had helped her make signs by nailing planks of scrap wood to stakes. NO TRESPASSING—he carved the angular letters using his prized Mora knife. The boys came through anyway, their bikes sputtering. Their voices were scratchy and warbling, not deep like this one.

She poked her head out of the opening. There were no other shoes but the boots. She looked up and saw a thin man. His face was in shadow. He wore a light-gray windbreaker and gray cap; from head to toe he was the color of the blanched trees around them.

Lumi crawled out and tugged the bottom of her fleece jacket down. "You're trespassing."

"I'm not."

She looked at her tepee and tried to identify the largest stick in the pile.

"If you're the Duffy girl, you own up to that creek. I closed on five acres here. That's the line." He slid a finger through the air, tracing the route of the creek.

She said nothing. She didn't know which of them was trespassing. She'd only ever seen her brother this deep in the woods.

"I'm Jack," he said.

She moved toward the stick she'd chosen and placed her hand on it.

"That's no shelter," he said. "If you're ever lost in the woods, or anywhere without a roof and four walls, and you go and build something half-assed like this, I'm telling you right now you might as well not bother. You might as well invite the rain and wind to kill you."

He nudged the base of the tepee with the toe of his boot and half of it tumbled down.

She stared at the pile. She couldn't think of what to say, whether it should be angry or sarcastic, and what kind of words might combine to that effect. But he was already dragging over an enormous dead branch, pulling and stomping on it until he'd broken it down to a six-foot piece. "This is your ridgepole," he said. "This is about the size that would fit you, the length of you, lying with your arms over your head. I'd need a longer one myself, but this'll do for a pip-squeak."

In the grove was a stump where Ty had cut down an old, mostly dead ash tree years ago. Now Jack set one end of the pole on the stump and the other end on the ground. He grabbed an armful of the tepee branches and began leaning them against the pole along either side. "This is the ribbing," he said.

She sat down in the leaves and watched him work. He was the same height as her father, but much leaner. When he took off his windbreaker and rolled up his sleeves, his exposed arms were browner than his face.

She twirled a leaf in the dirt. "Gonna take all day?" she asked.

Jack laughed but did not answer. When he was finished with the frame, he scooped up leaves and smaller twigs and began piling them on top. Some of the debris fell through, but most of it stayed. "Get on over and help already," he said.

She stood up and kicked some leaves toward the structure. He swept those into his jacket and added them to the pile. She kicked again, and once in a while bent to scoop the leaves into her arms. Her fleece jacket was too small for her, so she peeled it off and left it on the ground. Soon they'd cleared all the nearby leaves; around them was a bare circle of dirt. For all that work, the shelter was not very impressive. It was just a pile of leaves and sticks. Yet it was a kind of secret; from twenty yards away, a person could have glanced right at it and not known she was seeing anything at all.

"At least two feet," he said. "You want to pile this up two feet high. This is your insulation." He rubbed a maple leaf between his fingers. "The good stuff. You'll want it inside, too. The ground's a heat sink—sucks your heat right away. Shove as much as will fit in there, then get inside and compress it, and shove in more, and compress it, and shove in more. Only then—" He suddenly dropped so they were face-to-face. He was brown and gray all over, but his eyes were pale and blue. "Only then can you allow yourself to sleep."

He had left an opening in the shelter. Now he picked up her fleece, zipped it closed, and stuffed the floppy torso full of leaves. He tied the sleeves together, creating a tidy pillow. "This'll be your door plug. For now. Remember—door faces away from the wind." He created two more piles of leaves and a pile of twigs by the door.

"Crawl inside feet first," he said.

She chewed on the inside of her cheek. She could go home to her empty house, or she could enter this small, shabby cave. She squatted. She shimmied in on her belly. The leaves inside rustled, but the shelter itself did not move. It was sturdy.

"Is there any light in there? Besides what's coming from the door?"

"Nope." It was dark, soft, dry. She was in a small bubble of air in an enormous leaf pile. She thought she heard a whispering—the murmuring of the woods.

"Compress the leaves. Flatten them beneath you." He shoved a pile of leaves into the shelter. "Now add another layer," he said, and she did.

He explained something about how the door was the weakest point, but it was hard to concentrate on his words. He stuffed her fleece pillow into the entrance, and they shoved leaves against it, she from inside and he from outside. She knew it was daylight out, but where she lay it was perfectly black. She could hear herself exhale. The smallest of her movements caused the leaves to crackle. It was the dead of night, or she had gone blind, or all light had drained from the world.

"You could spend the night in there," he said, his voice dampened. "No sleeping bag, nothing. And you'd come out alive."

Lumi lay unmoving, imagining nightfall, snowfall, all kinds of things fallen while she was tucked away. When she pushed the door to the side and slid back out, Jack was gone. The sky was an inky blue with a single coral slash across it. She brushed herself off and went home.

THE NEXT DAY, SHE BUILT a new shelter, farther down the creek. She stayed on the side that Jack claimed to own. It took her two or three times as long, but when she was finished with the hideaway, she was pleased. It looked just like the first one. She lay inside, and when she grew bored of that, she whacked a nearby tree trunk with a stick. Two crows shot into the sky.

Finally Jack appeared. Without speaking, he studied her work. He was wearing the same boots, pants, hat, windbreaker.

"Not bad," he said. "I'd trim this bit, though," he said, tapping the part of the ridgepole that stuck out from the pile. "If it rains, this'll lead the water right to your head."

She shrugged.

"It could kill you," he said. "Just being wet. Hypothermia." He paused. "Want to see a shelter I built? It's a different kind, a dugout. It's not too far, just back this way half a mile."

He began walking fast. He didn't turn around to check on her. She followed him to the creek, nearly running, and they made their way along its bank into an area of the woods she hadn't explored before. There were fewer trees and more brush. Dry, leafless vines and branches grew low along the ground in tangles.

He stopped in front of a dirt mound covered with brush and leaves. He reached into the thickest part of it and a whole piece came away. Lumi made fists to hide her delight. It was a hatch door, made with two layers of woven twigs and vines and filled in with leaf debris. The door revealed an opening into a canoe-shaped space. There was a mattress of leaves on the floor. An empty can of beans lay on its side.

"Haven't you got a house?" she asked.

"I do."

"Why don't you live there?"

He shrugged and crouched, preparing to enter the shelter. "I'm practicing."

"For what?"

He stopped and stared at her. "Wish I knew."

FOR DINNER LUMI ASSEMBLED a sandwich of sliced bread and bologna. Except for the kitchen, the house was dark. With her sandwich in one hand, she walked through both floors, flipping on the lights. She avoided the closed door, behind which her father was resting.

He'd wake in a few hours and leave for his night shift at the hospital pharmacy. She knew he was slumped in his desk chair, hands on the armrests, eyes open but pupils shrunken to poppy seeds. He'd be blinking slowly, as though his eyelids were fighting gravity both ways. She couldn't push away the conviction that a spirit had strayed in from the woods and commandeered his body. A tired spirit, one that had been adrift. Even when her father was moving around the house, he was barely aware of her. When he washed his hands, he seemed to be preparing for some weighty, exhausting task; his breaths came slow and shallow. Before he left at night, he turned and scanned the interior of the house as if trying to relearn it. She often hid from him.

But tonight she waited for him at the door. "I'm going to camp outside," she declared.

He scratched his lower jaw, four fingernails scraping stubble. "You've got school tomorrow, and I won't be home."

She dug her fingernails into the flesh of her palms. She shouldn't have mentioned it. He wouldn't have known if she'd just gone.

"Next week," he said. "When I'm off. We'll rummage the basement for the…" He searched for the word. "…tent. Some camping, fresh air, it'll be just the thing."

They'd never gone camping before and never would. It was her mother who had told her where the patches of poison ivy grew, her mother who'd pressed flowers and leaves in his massive pharmacology books, staining the thin, translucent pages. Once they had buried a rotted pumpkin in a sunny spot; new vines reached out from the earth, crawled along the ground, and birthed brash flowers and misshapen fruit. And her mother had not been surprised.

Her mother had died while they were at school. Ty had found her. Walking up the driveway that afternoon, Lumi had seen only the edge of a stretcher pushed into an ambulance. Cardiomyopathy, her father said once, and she'd remembered the word ever since. Such a word, meaning your heart was scarred but you didn't know it.

That night, something had awakened her. She screamed, "Mom! Come here!" Immediately she realized her mother was gone, but she couldn't stop the wanting. "Come here now! Now!" she screeched, until both Ty and her father tore into her room.

The next night, it happened again. And again. They entered a loop in which she wailed, her father looked on with a strange intensity and Ty said, "Stop it, you're killing Dad." He lay flat on the floor beside her bed. Her father spread apart his hands as though to show her—nothing, there was nothing there, nothing left. No one could sleep. Her father brought home pills. He and Ty slept through the nights, and sometimes through the mornings. Only Lumi was awake. "Put me to sleep, too," she begged.

"You're too little for these," her father said.

WHILE HER FATHER WAS AT WORK, Lumi slept in the woods. She'd become an expert at building the shelters quickly, within an hour or two, and the next step was to test them. After a few desperately cold nights, she learned to construct them to be windproof. She hadn't known what it was like, to build your dwelling with your own hands. She had to scrounge for every last bit of it. In her burrows she lay very still, listening to the wind or animals agitating the leaves. The occasional mourning dove sounded its low, searching call, its five-note question. After dusk, how chilling and dark it became, how endless a night. She lay there blind until the darkness became less dark, which meant morning had finally come.

Jack appeared now and then. It always seemed to her that she'd been waiting for him, and that he'd been searching for her in the woods. He showed her how to make a friction fire. The first few times she tried, she couldn't even get the wood to smoke, and blisters sprouted across her palms. But she became stronger and better at holding the piece of drill wood in place while spinning it with her handmade bow.

"Look," Jack said, pointing at her head. "You're steaming."

She looked up and saw misty threads rising from his wool cap.

"Like a boiling kettle, your head," he said. "Now hold that still. I think your head's going to catch fire before that wood so much as warms."

She scowled to keep from smiling.

Jack was different from the fifth-grade boys. They were always pushing people and pretending to stumble and saying disgusting things. They all looked the same, in T-shirts, sweatpants, untied high-top sneakers.

She used to be friends with a boy named Gary, who wore collared shirts and glasses. They spent whole afternoons throwing things at a huge pine tree in his yard, trying to get them to land on its high, ample boughs. Forks and hairbrushes and shoes that belonged to Gary's sister. But after Lumi's mother died, dinners at Gary's were intolerable. His mother would ask, "Do you eat dinner at home? Every night? How many chairs are at your dining table?"

In the mornings, Lumi slipped into the house before her father returned. If she had school, she took a shower. If not, she waited for her father to go to sleep before heading back out again.

She made fires. She ground acorns with rocks and leached them in water. She pulled up grass and ate the tiny white part above the roots. She even caught a scrawny grasshopper—the last holdout of autumn—and removed its antennae, wings, and legs before cooking it on a flat stone by the fire. All she could stomach was a piece the size of her pinky nail. She thought of how Jack had scolded her once—she'd made a gagging noise when he talked about snaring a small bird for a snack.

At dawn, she crept out of her shelter and used her bandanna to wipe dew from the leaves and grass. She carefully wrung out the few drops into her water bottle, then went back to collecting more. It was a painstaking process, and the water did not taste clean. She built shelters all over the woods and created fire from wet, dry, hard, and soft wood, practicing and practicing.

"Shelter, fire, water, food," Jack had said. "Keep your priorities in that order. You can get by three days without water and three weeks without food. But you might not live three hours without a warm place to sleep."

TY CAME HOME FOR FOUR DAYS over Thanksgiving break. Lumi found him in the kitchen making spaghetti, moving from stove to sink to counter as though he had never left. His wide shoulders were hunched and his big blond head bent over a pot of sauce. "Hey, peanut," he said with his mouth full, and tapped her nose.

After the spaghetti, they made milkshakes with chocolate syrup. Ty had gone grocery shopping. As they ate, she gave him survival pointers. The next day, she took him out to see her very best shelter. He jerked his chin at it. "I wonder if it'd really hold up."

"Hold up?"

"If you slept in it."

Lumi tilted her head as if considering the answer.

They gathered pine cones and she showed him how to extract the nuts. "These are a lot smaller than at the store," he said.

She nodded. "They're still a net positive in terms of calories spent and earned."

"That right?" He gazed at the pine nuts in his hand.

On Thanksgiving Day, he made her his sous chef; she was allowed to execute the best tasks, like shucking corn, painting the turkey with honey, pushing a masher through the potatoes.

Ty licked the masher. "It's missing something."

She shrugged. Their mother had cheated by dumping in a packet of onion dip, but he wouldn't know that.

They set the dining table with china and filled wine glasses to the top with Cran-Apple juice.

"Wow," their father said. "Now who did what? What did you put in the corn? Nothing? Really nothing? It's fantastic." When Ty thrust a turkey leg at him, he cried, "Look at that color!"

Ty dropped the leg on his plate from a distance.

"There's sugar in the carrots," Lumi said, and grinned when her father spooned up a serving. His eyebrows were stiff with effort.

Dessert was her favorite—a pie filled with Cool Whip, cream cheese, and crushed Butterfingers—but it meant dinner was coming to an end. She ate two slices as slowly as she could.

Lumi heard them on the stairs that night. Ty was shouting. "Did you know I have a girlfriend? She invited me home for Thanksgiving."

Ty was stocky and short; he'd have to stand one step up to be on eye level with their father. Their father said little or nothing. The front door opened and slammed.

While Lumi lay in bed, her father came up the stairs, light-footed. She closed her eyes and felt his wispy presence in the doorway. The wandering spirit from the woods. It gazed at her as though she were a figurine or a photograph. The footsteps retreated to the bedroom. She heard the rattle of the plastic bottle. Hydrocodone, she'd read on the label. For his trouble with his teeth.

She was having a hard time staying awake. It was the heat. She was no longer accustomed to indoor heating; grogginess pressed in. Sandwiched between the mattress and thick down comforter, which settled into her contours and fluffed and sighed when she shifted, she gave in to the heavy warmth.

She woke to Ty nudging her. She could see the outline of his sizable chin. "What?"

"You . . . don't spend all your time outside with that man."

She sat up. "No one does anything wrong."

"I know."

"You don't sound like you know."

Her bedroom windows faced the woods but the blinds were down. She could only hear the woods. It was gusty out, and the tops of the trees were thrashing, unleashing a sound like a storm of insects.

He straightened her covers, then sat by her feet. "I asked around. He does know a lot of things. He used to work as a naturalist in a state park—the guy who leads field trips and, you know, writes pamphlets that tell you the names of trees and birds. But you've got to be careful. Things have happened to him."

"What things?"

"I don't know much. He had a wife before, but she died."

Lumi tried to pull her comforter up. It wouldn't budge.

"He bought land out here by us, but no one's seen any house."

ONE OVERCAST MORNING, she slept through the sunrise. She picked off the leaves that stuck to her fleece and headed home.

"Where'd you go?" Her father was standing in the doorway of the bathroom. He scratched his neck and squinted at her as though trying to see through dirty glass.

"I camped out," she said.

"You found the tent."

Lumi ducked her head.

"Did you take the lantern? Take the lantern. It's got a good handle." He was slurring a bit, but she knew what he was talking about: an electric lamp he'd bought for her mother, who liked to sit out on summer nights. He'd sometimes join her, back when he used to work the day shift and spend evenings at home. Lumi remembered her mother sitting with her legs curled up on the folding chair. The sound of her father eating apples.

That afternoon, digging around in the basement, she found the lantern, along with the tent. They were crammed in an open box with her mother's gardening tools. Lumi shook dust from the tent and lantern and carried both out to the woods. She shoved them into an old debris shelter she no longer used, and plugged up the entrance again.

THE GROUND WAS DAMP and alive with loitering specks of white. It was the first snow. Ty would be home again soon, for a whole week.

"Teach me a snow trench," she said to Jack.

Jack laughed. "There's not enough for that."

They crouched by a single-log fire in the late afternoon. Lumi prodded it with a stick, though it didn't need tending.

"I've got two things to tell you," he said. "First is, merry Christmas." He opened his backpack and threw something purple at her. She unfolded it. It was a waterproof shell, and it fit her exactly. She zipped it all the way up so that the long collar closed around her mouth. She cinched the hood. Only a strip of her face was exposed.

"You look like a cartoon space kid," he said.

"What's the other thing?" she asked through the collar.

"I'm leaving."

She blinked. "What do you mean?"

"I'm off."

"Where?"

"Around the country."

"The whole country?"

"Don't know yet."

"When will you know?"

"When I'm someplace else."

"Are you coming back?"

He toed a branch. "Maybe."

She turned her face upward. The sky was dingy, its blue leaking away, but where that color went was a mystery. She pulled the drawstrings on her hood even tighter and stuck her hands in the vinyl pockets, burrowing into herself. She knew Jack could move through the forests and never spend a single dollar. He could live anywhere there were mountains or woods, and no one would know where he was. He could just vanish.

After a while, he stood up, gracefully and silently, without using his hands at all. He looked down at her, and his mouth made the shape of a clumsy smile. "A snow trench isn't so different from a dugout. Want to give a dugout a shot?"

She thought about saying no. "A dugout like yours?"

"Sure," he said.

"Next to yours?"

"All right."

Lumi led the way. They trudged along the creek. When they reached Jack's hideaway, they walked around it in a circle.

"Look for a natural dent in the ground," he said. "Saves energy." He pointed to a depression with a stick. "Like this," he said. "And then we just deepen it."

They went to work hollowing it out, trying different sticks and rocks until they found something they liked. Lumi used a flat, pointed stone, small enough that she could drag it along the dirt over and over again without tiring too quickly. Jack wielded a large rock with one hand.

When they were finished, he said, "That didn't take very long at all. Good thing you're so short. Less to dig."

The result was a five-foot-long ditch in the ground, parallel to Jack's. She lay lengthwise in it and felt like a pill in a foil tab.

"Now the roof," he said. They stacked rows of branches across the top. Next they threw leaves and pine needles over it, and finally all the dirt they had dug up. He made a hatch door for the opening.

"When are you leaving?" she asked.

"Crack of dawn, my friend."

When night came, he made a fire by their dugouts and cooked a can of Spam. She did not leave and he did not ask her to. While they ate, the snow began to fall in bigger clumps, and she opened her mouth to let them in because the Spam was hot and salty. Everything in the woods grew dusty and pale.

"You cold?" he asked.

"The jacket's good."

Afterward, she slid into her dugout. She left the hatch door off and peered out from the hole, studying the barren trees that were fuzzed with snow. One tree still clung to its dead, quavering leaves.

She lifted her head to watch Jack, but he wasn't doing much, just squatting and pushing things around with his rock. He didn't need to prepare for his journey, she realized, because he didn't have any belongings. When it became too cold, she pulled the door closed. He stayed outside, rustling. Sometime later, she heard him move his own hatch door. She could tell when he settled on his mattress of leaves.

He was so close, lying parallel to her in the ground three feet away. His heat seemed to seep through the soil between them. She thought of her mother. A bug was crawling on her neck, or maybe it was just a tickle. The night went on, black and long and crackling. She couldn't sleep, buried like this beside him.

"What time will you leave?" she asked again.

"Before you get up." He sounded far away but awake. "You warm?"

It wasn't that she couldn't believe it, the fact of his leaving; she understood it well.

"I said, are you warm?"

"No," she said. In a way, it was true.

She thought he had fallen asleep. Finally he said, "Come on in." He said it so quietly she could have chosen not to hear it.

When she entered, she had to feel her way to him. One hand on the firm, compressed leaves, one hand patting his boot. The mattress was sized just for him, but he turned on his side to make room. She lay down, leaving a sliver of space between them. He curled around her with his whole body.

Somehow he smelled more like fire than fire itself—more woodsy and bitter and burned.

That scent, his heat, the sweet rot of leaves—they sank her into sleep, and she couldn't surface. Later, replaying the night, it seemed to her that he'd asked, as she was drifting farther and farther away, "Are you still cold? Are you asleep? Are you warm now?"

When she woke, Jack was gone. She wrapped her arms around herself, hugging her new jacket. She'd tried so hard to stay awake. Not that it would have mattered; she knew she was not enough to keep back a man who was going.

Outside the dugout, snow lay thick on the ground and every bare, reaching branch of every tree held a strip of white.

She wanted to call for Jack in the woods. He might still be nearby. She would frighten away the birds and send the ground creatures into hiding, cutting through the fresh snow with her reedy voice. But the call and answer would be like the doves, always—Where? Where? Where? She spent the morning trudging through the snow, stamping out aimless paths. She looked for other tracks but saw only her own, leading nowhere. She returned to Jack's dugout. Lying on his mattress of leaves now, she could spread her arms and legs. He might come back. He might lift open the door this very instant and toss a twig at her head, disapproving of her idleness.

She stayed on, leaving only to forage for bits of food or build a fire. She spoke to no one, not even herself.

AROUND DUSK ON THE SECOND NIGHT, she heard a call. A word. Her name.

Jack! He was back for her. Lying in his dugout, she whispered, "Hello." She said it again, louder, more cheerful. It hurt her throat to speak, like peeling a seal off her larynx.

He called again. It was Ty. She'd forgotten he was coming. The shouts were dulled by snow, and then they were gone, leaving only wind. A long while later she heard a skittering, like a piece of gravel skipping across a road. A wood spirit, she thought, come to claim her body. She was ready for it.

Let it plunge its spongy arms down her throat and shrug on her tight skin. It would grasp for something in her, the very last bit of her, a final scant thing the size and hardness of a cherry pit.

"Lumi!" The voice was crumbly and far away.

Ty was searching for her, here in the woods. The warmth that surged through her was almost painful. She threw open the door and sprang out. She ran in the direction of their house, kicking up the loose, clean snow. She saw the back of Ty's stooped figure, paused in the gloom between two aspens, and charged. He stumbled forward.

"You," he said, turning around. He squeezed her face hard between his palms.

"How long are you staying?"

"A whole week." One corner of his mouth slid up. It was not a real smile. It never was.

She kicked him hard in the shins. His thick arms closed around her.

"Can't you take me with you?" she asked. A gust blasted them, and she curled her fingers around the bottom edge of his coat.

"Jesus, it's cold." He was panting. "Where've you been?"

"Camping."

"I thought Dad was crazy. You really did? In this weather?"

"I know how to stay warm."

"But I didn't see the tent. I looked all over."

"I don't have a tent." She smashed her face into his cold, plasticky coat.

"No tent?" He pulled away to assess her. Her hood had fallen back, and her cheeks and ears ached. She tried to embrace him again, but he pushed her away, and she fell onto her hands. She nearly cried from the surprise of it, the burn of snow on her palms.

"Take me with you," she said.

He lifted his face so she couldn't see his eyes. Above them, the brittle trees gazed down.

Dorothea Lasky

A HOSPITAL ROOM

Morning walking is like a hospital room

The getting up and feeling sorry for sleep

Putting my fat body into a cab and going to the hospital

The smell of soup and pus everywhere

Not telling hardly anyone for fear they'd kill my child like I almost had

Listening to my headphones, dreaming of surprise

Little ego in the hospital, does it care where you've been

We carry status, but it doesn't care

Still it pays for you to have an expensive room

And the nurses and everyone, they treat you better

A little extra cot, in the jail cell where they let you stay

And maybe the doctor is more interested to save you

If you flash some cash out your dressing gown

And it's winter, so you wash the stitches in Vaseline

Bathe the raw skin in marijuana, these things

Eat turmeric because inflammation is

And the cells, they keep spilling

Or really, nothing more blank than your lifeforce

Or the promise of it

So you pray to that

Pray for that

Do you hear me

In the morning touching the wrist you will know

His cold bald head in the winter air

How I wanted to rub it on my hands and kiss it

Instead I had to let him fly from tree to tree

Eagle wrapped around this disaster for so many years

Nothing more unnerving than being a thing

Explorer in his fancy mud

Oh Behold, Behold

Scapegoat Child

—

KATHLEEN COLLINS

I n the crucible of our family my sister burned like molten steel. Once I saw her arms outspread her legs hanging limp and useless wet saliva dripping from her tongue. I screamed they surrounded her lifted her onto the sheets where she convulsed for hours traces of stain and guilt shattering her face my sister my sister cunning participant spectator victim inside the ugly family circle.

Her name was Josephine. No shortening to a rounder, softer sound like *Josie* or *Jo* was ever allowed her name was Josephine. Wide eyes alert for trouble a mouth that protruded too far lips too full for comfort. A skinny knock-kneed girl who stared so hard one day her eyes crossed locked and the full lips took on a slight tremor.

Her room was on the top floor a tiny place with a wooden ceiling that stared down at her. Yellow roses in her bedspread. A shiny dark floor at her feet. In the mornings she came to life early pounced awake before us ran to perch outside our door.

Her thin legs hop out of bed eyes crossed alert she slips down the stairs in the morning stillness. We are all asleep while she listens and waits. Who will greet her when the door opens who will smile give up the first of their morning love? Our father trips over her small body on his way to the bathroom. Through the crack in the door she watches our slow momma fall on her knees to pray.

She sits and waits. No one comes to lift her in their arms. The day is over. But tomorrow she will begin again, early early even earlier.

At breakfast she will not eat. Her head falls back eyes disappear deep inside their sockets while we watch. An angry mob of three we watch and wait. Then she comes back slowly her head comes forward eyes slip back into place she giggles a silly burble that pushes her lips out too far. Then our father sends her reeling a hard slap with all his might until the burble is gone she sits staring cross-eyed at the three of us a twisted smile jutting out her lips.

The day my father married my mother my sister was three years old. She trotted to the ceremony on skinny wings a beaky little bird pinned down by other memories, an earlier womb ancient kisses that sent her to bed and woke her up. Perched high on ancient shoulders she watched our father join himself to the pretty woman with the long old maid's eyes the stiff cheeks and black hair piled high high high on her head. A balmy September day bright blue with trees and sky and Josephine sitting atop her perch like a beaky bird sniffing the air for an old melody a plumper rounder mommy once a plumper rounder mommy who sat by a window and died just sat by a window and died.

They lift her down she threads her skinny legs around our father's tall unbending frame climbing frantically to reach his face seek one last embrace before this balmy day tramples her to death. I had a mommy once didn't I have a mommy once. Nobody answers. The pretty lady with the black hair smiles a mute and frozen smile the skinny child is handed back to ancient arms that fold her one last time.

There is a room that lives in her memory large and blue where someone comes in at night to read to her. There is a cozy chair thick with cushions beside an open window and a glass for her to fetch water for the woman in the cozy chair. There is someone who says her name *Jo–se–phine* it has a laugh in it warm eyes a lap rocking back and forth. There is ... she sits up, spitefully awake a tiny hawk quivering on the edge of memory, where death confusion a host of uneasy comings and goings plague her, whispering women who stroked her hair a father with a shamed broken face a flight of steps she climbed on all fours nimbly up and down up and down she would not be still slipping in and out where grief reigned her shrill little arms flapping up and down.

The lady with the black hair puts her to bed. Are you my new mommy she asks are you my new mommy while a wooden ceiling stares down at her yellow roses drift in and out the window she stares at the lady with the pretty cheeks are you my new mommy she asks and the lady frowns a scolding look comes into her eyes I'm your mommy she answers her cheeks are tight the eyes too round. The child will not be still she squirms in the cold bed you're my new mommy she asks my new new mommy holding tight to the silent blue room the face that asks for a glass of water you're my new mommy she squirms her shrill little body will not be still.

OVER AGAINST THIS TALE is another, about the pretty lady with the high cheekbones about the shamefaced man with the tall unbending frame about love and the acting out of only the rituals of love about loss and grief and the old maid's eyes in the pretty woman's face and the sense of shame in the tall man's eyes. A family tale stretching its elusive fingers backward and forward until it finally reaches out to the skinny girl in her top-floor room.

The pretty lady's name is Letitia. She was thirty-eight when she came to mother the squirming child. Lace collars framed her round face with the too-round eyes her dresses were dark things that grated as she walked she had the bearing of a Sunday-school teacher a rigidity that fluttered beneath the bright gracious smile the sweet voice that trilled up and down something made of stone, an old maid's current already fixed immutable behind the well-meaning smile.

Letitia's mother's name was Sadie a big-boned woman with thick plaits hanging down her back silent eyes like an Indian. Her father's name was Hood he drank too much spent years beside his spittoon chewing tobacco and shrinking further further inside a drunken shell. She had one sister, Lavinia, a tiny slice brittle to look at frail hysterical attached to Letitia like an ant to an oak tree.

The tall unbending man is Roland. He was thirty-two to her thirty-eight, six years balanced by grief a squirming child a newborn. Six years a distance held in check by his persuasive manner. He presented himself well handsome strict in his bearing a strong argumentative tone in his voice. Beneath the smooth-riding surface was chaos pure unaccountable chaos a swarming beehive of fury and grief.

His father's name was Jeremy a nearsighted madman raging against his five sons storms that demolished the house scattered the children left a hollow wailing at the center of each of them. His mother, Ella, was a large woman with thick mahogany hair scooped tight in a bun. Stern implacable an immovable object at the center of Jeremy's myopic lashings.

All these folk are Negroes what dark brooding what hopeless feelings underpin the already cruel family landscape who can say but all these folk are Negroes.

Death fits in the picture a handsome woman with no trace of sternness a cool smile on her lips and brow death fits in the picture the abrupt cessation of a sweet potent struggle with life death fits in the picture and a momma a momma God in heaven bless the seamless connection of a momma.

IT'S JOSEPHINE WE CHOSE to carry our wounds grow cross-eyed burbled confused pins sticking out from all sides it's Josephine we chose with her shrill cries and gestures her convulsive goings-on it's Josephine we chose.

Wound tighter than a drum beating the air with her fists she screams for our father Daddy she screams I don't want to take a nap don't make me take a nap a hollow flapping of wings to beat away his absence beat away the round eyes that stare and wait I don't want to take a nap she screams her little wings convulse out of one crossed eye she watches I don't want to take a nap she screams the round eyes turn to stone only pain is left she wishes she could be still only pain is left she wishes she could be still.

Instead she yelps flaps her wings ceremonies dance in her head Letitia becomes the injured party.

The house is quiet sunlight wanders in and out the baby sleeps. Josephine climbs out of bed to watch it this tiny thing silent and serene she takes its hand its little fingers move back and forth she touches its face the eyes do not open she climbs into the crib nestles her squirming body beside the flesh free of memory and sleeps.

Who watches over a new lady in stiff dresses pretty red lips round eyes dim and lackluster she moves from room to room up and down the corridors of a new house broken off from the past. A new lady watches over unaccustomed to children to our father's emphatic presence to strange rooms free of Sadie and Hood. A new lady watches over a thin grating when she walks a sweetened whisper when she talks a new lady watches over dull patina for our glossy hysteria.

The house is quiet. Josephine sleeps beside the baby, Letitia sits crocheting in the afternoon sun. The front door opens before he can cross the threshold Josephine comes to life slips screaming down the stairs into his arms. Roland looks. Letitia appears at the doorway. The child begins to do things her eyes begin to roll her head bobs back and forth the child begins to do things. Roland looks. Letitia stands in the doorway. The child keeps doing things sticks out her tongue shrieks and quivers like a useless monkey the child keeps doing things. Roland looks. Letitia stands in the doorway. The child keeps doing things sticks out her tongue shrieks and quivers like a useless monkey the child keeps doing things. Roland looks. Letitia stands in the doorway. The child keeps doing things a tiny cauldron growing bright before their eyes Roland reaches out lifts her in his arms carries her up to her room. The baby is awake he shuts the door sits down on the yellow roses begins to speak a mother was needed a mother his face crumples guilt and grief control him a mother was needed a mother he begins to cry. The room is still Josephine stops her squirming, at ease at last behind the closed door, drifting inside his familiar smell of grief and misunderstanding at ease at last in this petrified place where just the three of them may go only the three of them may go.

WOUNDED IN HER BODY she carried our pain wars were fought a bloody field emerged wounded in her body she carried our pain darting in and out of the shadows like a small soldier.

Nothing grew between Letitia and Roland. Walls went up the house locked from the inside nothing moved. All motion came from Josephine. Thumb stuck to her lips her body twitching all motion came from Josephine.

She was always underfoot turning herself into a smoke screen of nervous faults and failings, a weeding ground that we could rake and pull.

She was always underfoot in the heat of battle she would fight on both sides help Letitia to her feet pummel Roland's advancing body with her tight little fists.

She was always underfoot a squirming reminder of dead memories and dreams.

Then one day she burst. Her little legs flew apart her stubborn arms took to the sky her head rattled and shook her overworked eyes fled from their sockets a sudden restless wind was blowing her apart too many wars had been fought on her soil too many wars had been fought on her soil she would not be still. Together they must pin her down. Together the pretty lady with the stiff eyes the warm daddy connected backward in time must pin her down until their uneasy union jells in her body.

Mónica de la Torre

BOXED IN

Heads up, false friends use familiarity as camouflage.

In the source language *deciduous* might be confused with *apathy*,

but nothing could be further away from *desidia* than the timed impermanence
of leaves.

Yes, even forests engage in a form of family planning.

We took for granted the tree outside our window until it failed to bud.

A ginkgo, they cut it down when the building across the street went up.

Since our view is limited, we like to imagine the situation from the missing
tree's perspective.

Given the recent turn of events, it might have resisted blooming.

It was protesting its decorative use to boost property values.

Or perhaps after millennia of honing its particulars, it refused "the magic
of tree-lined streets."

Concrete blocks these social beings' access to fungal networks,

prevents their roots from interconnecting.

Are you a reluctant loner like the specimens that surround us here today?

I hope you understand I don't mean to ruin the relationship.

The Art of Fiction No. 238

———

ELENA
PONIATOWSKA

Elena Poniatowska is one of the few sur-
vivors of her generation of Mexican
writers, which includes Carlos Fuentes,
José Emilio Pacheco, and Carlos Monsiváis. In
Mexico, she is most often called "Elenita"—
perhaps dismissively years ago, but now with all
the affection and respect a diminutive can imply.
Her name is a byword throughout the Spanish-
speaking world, though English-language readers
know her only from the small percentage of her
work that has been translated. Her more than forty
books encompass a great many genres ("though
not science fiction," she quips); she is best known
for fiction and nonfiction based on interviews
"collaged," as she puts it, into a seamless whole
with a skill that reminds one of Sergei Eisenstein's
Battleship Potemkin.

Poniatowska's focus is almost exclusively on the most marginalized of Mexicans: women and the poor, who, together, make up more than half the population. She has chronicled oppression and military brutality (*La noche de Tlatelolco* [*Massacre in Mexico*, 1971]) and natural disaster coupled with government corruption (*Nada, nadie: Las voces del temblor* [*Nothing, Nobody: The Voices of the Mexico City Earthquake*, 1988]), as well as the daily lives of the working class in novels such as *Hasta no verte Jesús mío* (*Here's to You, Jesusa!*, 1969). For her outspokenness, she has been placed under police surveillance ("certainly not for my protection") and jailed twice, though briefly.

She is now eighty-five and, having been diagnosed with cardiac illness, has agreed to take things easier to avoid hospitalization. But it is impossible to imagine this famously energetic woman putting her feet up. In fact, she has not. She maintains a demanding schedule of lecturing and remains a working journalist, while at the same time completing a biography of Stanisław Poniatowski, the last king of Poland, from whose brother she is descended. In 2013, Poniatowska was awarded the Cervantes Prize, the most prestigious literary award in the Spanish-speaking world.

In a country in which most people of means engage domestic help, Poniatowska shops, cooks, pays her own bills, and employs no secretary. She has lived in the Chimalistac neighborhood of Mexico City for more than twenty-five years, in a modest, book-filled house. It is there that we met for our two principal interviews in 2013, later supplemented by emails and conversations on the phone; we spoke in English. She arrived to our first session straight from an event at the British embassy, yet immediately ready to begin.

—*Stephen Kurtz*

INTERVIEWER

So many of your books, fiction and nonfiction, are explorations of the lives of very poor people. What makes it possible for you to cross the boundaries of social class so gracefully?

PONIATOWSKA

I think of the Surrealist painter and writer Leonora Carrington. She was my great friend and I wrote a novel about her, called *Leonora* (2011). She was born into an upper-class English family and was even presented to the queen, though she took along Huxley's *Eyeless in Gaza* to pass the time waiting in the line of debutantes. Typically, young women of her class were expected to marry someone rich and titled, but she rebelled almost from childhood, was expelled from two schools, and finally found her way to a good art school. Then she encountered Surrealism, especially in the work of Max Ernst. She was drawn to him even before she met him. Then they did meet, and they lived and worked together in the South of France. But after the Nazis invaded, Ernst, who was Jewish, was arrested by the Gestapo. Carrington was devastated and fled to Spain. Her state of mind became critical, and she had a breakdown at the British embassy in Madrid. Perhaps her "madness" was really a sort of sanity, because she was horrified by the developing war, by the cruelty she was seeing all around her, by the treatment of the Jews—all of which she either foresaw or was evident to her before it became obvious to "sane" people. And so she was confined to an asylum, in Santander, for the upper classes—because, she reminds me, upper-class people can be crazy, too—although it was hardly a holiday. It was a terrible but also transforming experience. Out of it, she wrote *Down Below* and painted works that expressed her experience.

Carrington escaped confinement in Lisbon with the help of a Mexican diplomat there. She went first to New York and then to Mexico, where she continued to live, marrying Imre Weisz, with whom she had two children. She was a wonderful mother to those children and a treasure for Mexico and for me.

INTERVIEWER

Is Carrington, then, the very sort of person you admire for having crossed class boundaries?

PONIATOWSKA

She made a decision to live her own life and not the life that was expected of her. Or perhaps she followed a vocation more than she made a decision. I am filled with admiration for her integrity—defending it against the rules of a social class that prevented gifted people from becoming all that they had in them to become. Carrington never gave in.

INTERVIEWER

And Elena?

Well, there are some obvious affinities but also significant differences between us. She is something of a hero to me, but who is a hero to himself, after all? She defended her integrity from the beginning of her life in a very blunt way, which was not true of me. I tended to be obedient and unsure of myself. She always spoke out against injustice, which took me more time to understand and to find my own way of expressing. And while she was relatively self-confident, I am very aware of my weaknesses, as a person—especially in reviewing my life at this age—and as a writer. Spanish, after all, is not my first language. I was born in France and came to Mexico at nine years old. We spoke French at home, and I went first to the Colegio Windsor, where we were taught in the English manner, then to the French lycée, and afterward, for a few years, to Eden Hall, a convent boarding school of the Sacred Heart near Philadelphia—an order itself established in France. So I grew up as a French speaker, then learned English formally, but learned Spanish only from the household staff, which had an effect on my writing. Later on, though, I had help in improving it. To my regret, I never went to university. If I had been able to, I might have had a classical education, and I feel the lack of that. I had made a good beginning in Latin and would have studied and studied, and even completed a doctorate. As it is, I have had to work much harder than someone who has had a university education to write the sorts of things that might otherwise have come easily.

INTERVIEWER

Yet you have the ability to draw people out so that they tell you what really matters to them, something a university education cannot teach. And the gift of putting all those interviews together so that the book reads like an unbroken narrative, a page-turner, while at the same time preserving the unique qualities of each voice. Did you ever take writing workshops the way young writers do now?

PONIATOWSKA

I did win a scholarship for about a year to the Centro Mexicano de Escritores, founded by the wonderful American writer Margaret Shedd and originally supported by Rockefeller funds. There were only about seven of us meeting once a week, although the way it was structured, one had the opportunity to present one's own work only every couple months. It was an important institution that

At the typewriter, ca. 1956.

eventually published bibliographies and supported the publication of some books. Many important Mexican writers were in some way associated with it.

INTERVIEWER

Was that experience formative for you?

PONIATOWSKA

No. I learned, as they say, by doing. I began as an interviewer for the society pages of *Excélsior*—the only sort of thing a young woman could expect in those days. And despite having no experience, I was given the job because of my family and the entrée it gave me to society events. Since *Excélsior* is a daily paper, I had to produce these pieces every day with almost no time for review. Then I would read them in print and see that I had spent too much time on things of little importance and failed to ask about what mattered most. And so, with frequent embarrassment, that is how I learned. One also learns humility doing interviews, because people may not want to give you much time and so keep you waiting in an anteroom or are dismissive or in a bad mood, and all this has to be accepted. But I have come to understand that there is something about me of which I myself am unaware but that other people feel, something that allows them to talk more freely. Beyond that, both in the early days and later, I was helped by the fact that I am a small person, certainly compared to my sister, Kitzia, who is tall and statuesque. So people did not feel intimidated. Can you imagine if I had been a tall blonde with big tits?

INTERVIEWER

The image of Anita Ekberg just flashed across my mind.

In *La noche* you spoke to people who had just lost children, parents, spouses, and friends after the massacre of Tlatelolco. In *Nada, nadie*, you were deeply involved in the horrors of the 1985 quake, where people were suffering the same sorts of losses. Both of these books must have been emotionally wrenching and exhausting, yet you still found the energy to write and edit. What motivates you in doing this work?

PONIATOWSKA

In one important way, a Catholic childhood. When we were put to bed at night, we were always reminded that there were others who had no bed to sleep in and no food either, and that we had a responsibility to such people. So perhaps there is an element of guilt in all this.

INTERVIEWER

Guilt, it seems to me, is a rather weak motivation for creativity, and it's hard to imagine that guilt alone could have led you to produce so many books of such quality. In my own experience, people who have crossed class boundaries the way you have are also meeting a need within themselves—perhaps to be in contact with a grittier reality than the life into which they've been born.

I had not thought of that, but yes, I think you are right.

The pronoun *I* doesn't appear in your work, yet the most compelling of your nonfiction books have the quality of novels. And, despite the absence of *I*, you yourself are everywhere in these books, in your very decision to cover these events, in what you ask, and in what you choose to include or omit. But your personal reactions aren't stated—one might say that they are present and felt, but not declared.

That isn't the result so much of an ideological position. It's more my personality and, I imagine, my upbringing. I do not like to put myself forward. It's not that I wish to be an enigma to others, which is also a way of calling attention to oneself. I am simply more at ease in a role that does not put me in the foreground. There is also my family's sense of propriety in that. According to the way I was raised, one's name should appear in the papers only at birth, marriage, and death. People whose names appeared regularly were thought to be trying to sell something, which was seen as a kind of vulgarity.

I want to return for a moment to the ethos of Catholicism in your work, especially to the idea of responsibility for others that was part of your bedtime ritual as a child. Responsibility alone, as the parable of the Good Samaritan suggests, can be understood not as simply dutiful but as an action that proceeds from empathy. You can see it in your lifetime in the particularly French movement of worker priests, Emmanuel Mounier's "personalism," and the writings of Simone Weil.

I have read everything by Simone Weil, who was an extraordinary woman gifted with immense empathy. But I think she might have profited from some better advice. She was not physically strong and yet, in order to directly experience the struggle of working people, she undertook factory work that was too much for her. And she also fought in the Spanish Civil War and, being somewhat clumsy, stepped into a pail of boiling oil, was severely burned, and went to Portugal to recuperate. Later, she would eat only the minimal portion of food she believed was available to people in occupied France—a few potatoes perhaps. She had been diagnosed with tuberculosis, and this may well have contributed to her death.

INTERVIEWER

Then, as you see her, she is more of an inspiration than a model.

PONIATOWSKA

Yes, an inspiration. She could not have been a model for me because I am neither a genius nor a mystic and, like Leonora, I had children I loved and for whom I was responsible, so that even if I had discovered a vocation of this sort in myself, I could not have lived such an extreme life. And, beyond that, when I have blurred the line between myself as a person and as a writer, the writing has suffered.

INTERVIEWER

In what way?

PONIATOWSKA

I think *Nada, nadie* is not so good because, while I was gathering interviews and writing it, my house was also full of mattresses—I was putting people up who had been made homeless and making sandwiches for the ones camped out in the midst of that destruction. It was somehow possible to continue writing, but the quality of it was affected.

INTERVIEWER

Perhaps, in that instance, maintaining some sort of distance would simply not have been possible—perhaps not even moral. I think of the dilemma of war photographers, for example, who take pictures of horrors the world must know of yet can rarely intervene to help. Nick Ut, for example, the AP photographer who took the famous picture of a Vietnamese girl covered with burns, crying and running naked from her napalmed village. He did make sure that she was cared for, but that is not always possible, and, if a choice had to be made, maybe the picture would have had to be lost to us.

Yes, I suppose it was better to have written that book in the way I did than to have stood apart and done nothing. In any event, I could not have done that.

How did you arrive at your style of being a journalist?

I don't think there is much method in my imaginative writing—in the early novel *Lilus Kikus* (1954), for example, or, more recently, the story collection *Tlapalería* (*The Heart of the Artichoke*, 2003). Of course, imaginative writing always contains elements of the writer's lived experience, but there is a different sort of freedom in it than there is in reporting or in novels based on interviews. I try to write in a disciplined way, but a heavy schedule of conferences and traveling does not always make that possible. There is more method of a transmittable sort in work that is based on interviews. At the same time, it must be said, style, as I see it, is not an adornment added to a work. It is more, as Buffon said, that *"le style c'est l'homme même"*—style is the man himself. Let me find my copy of his *Discours*. Here. That famous line is actually the conclusion of a longer thought—"Writing well consists of thinking, feeling and expressing well, of clarity of mind, soul and taste." In my own words, I would say that style is a manifestation of the writer's being, which, of course, changes over time but retains something essential of who he is. I can look back at things I wrote years ago and still recognize myself in them, in the way sentences are constructed, the vocabulary, all of that and more. One does not develop a style. One develops oneself. Or, perhaps more accurately, one is born with a certain character and life shapes it. And then, if you write or paint or sculpt, you do those things with the person you have become. And that is style. And, of course, there is a certain development. If you look at early Rembrandt portraits, they are very linear and the brushstrokes are almost invisible. The late ones are much freer, and the brushstrokes are very obvious and as much a part of the work as the subject. These things are never intentional, and I cannot see how they can be explained.

Even so, I imagine people want to hear something less ineffable. After the first round of choosing, I must do a great deal of editing, since people are unburdening themselves to me, and, from the point of view of the needs of the book, rather than the needs of the person I'm interviewing, a great deal must be omitted. One man I interviewed for *Nada, nadie* was so unhappy with these omissions that he wrote his own book! I understand his feelings very well, but if I did not reduce long interviews to what feels to me to be their essence, I would end up with a chronicle—that is to say, something like a bad biography in which the biographer cannot bear to exclude anything he has learned in the course of his research. It might be a valuable record for historians but unreadable as a book. Even before this part of the process, I have

With David Alfaro Siqueiros in the Palacio de Lecumberri, then a prison, in 1960.

chosen the interviews that had the greatest visceral impact on me. It is not an intellectual choice. Then, after this editing comes the other sort of editing—the sort I have called "collagist" but which is better called "montagist."

INTERVIEWER

How did you develop your montagist technique?

PONIATOWSKA

By this point in the editing process, I have become thoroughly familiar with the material and have a sense of the sorts of statements that can establish a sequence or else can segue from one aspect of the subject to another. There cannot be a formula for doing this, and the process is never completed in one go. But there comes a point at which a flow has been established so that the book reads as a narrative that moves along at a readable pace, despite the differences in each voice. My own deepest interest as a writer is in fiction, but as I have learned, it is my work that is most socially engaged that is also the most valued by my readers. This happens to other writers. The American writer May Sarton, for example, thought of herself principally as a poet but is appreciated most for her journals. Here I must add that if I had been, say, a French writer, I would have been free to write whatever I wished, which would have been writing of an imaginative sort. But in Mexico, because of the suffering that is the result of centuries of corruption, there is a moral obligation to write of this. I could not ignore it, and, because I have become known for it and have refined my ability to write this way through practice, it became my principal work. At the same time that it could not have been otherwise, in looking back I feel an element of regret.

INTERVIEWER

All writing involves an interplay between style and method and habit. In your work, there is an unmistakably activist element, which is to say, the work itself is an action. Many aspects of your life from childhood on could be considered cosmopolitan. You are equally at home in French, English, and Spanish. You have read widely in European literatures. The people you have written about are often Mexican by choice—Leonora Carrington and Tina Modotti, for example. Which is all to say, you might have worked without regard for nationality, but instead nationality is critical to your work. How did that come about?

PONIATOWSKA

It was a decision. I came here as a young girl from France, as I have said, and, despite my mother's ancestry—she was a member of the Amor family, prominent in Mexico's landed aristocracy—the family was more oriented toward France than Mexico. I became a Mexican citizen only in 1969, though I still had French citizenship for a few more years. But I wanted very much to have roots, and I felt the only possibility of that was here in Mexico, where, in fact, I had already put down roots since coming back from Philadelphia. This was an evolution, of course. The society world I knew as a young woman, writing for *Excélsior*, was, as you say, cosmopolitan. Then, as now, the Jockey Club was a center of society, and I covered events there. As a social center, it was functionally no different than its counterparts in England or France. In that sense, these elite groupings are international since it is class membership rather than nationality that counts. If you look at the membership of the Jockey-Club de Paris, for example, you will find many of the same names that appear in Saint-Simon—La Rochefoucauld, Montesquiou, the duc de Luynes, for example. In most cases, the real power of these people disappeared years ago, after the various revolutions, yet they retain a certain tribalism. At the same time, it is impossible to find one's roots as a Mexican—or, for that matter, as a French person—if you remain enclosed within the boundaries of that tribe. Boundaries, after all—of custom, of language, of what is and is not permitted—not only function to keep others out but also keep those inside from expanding. The name Poniatowska—*ska* for women, *ski* for men, with parallels in all Slavic languages—is recognized in France but in Mexico it meant nothing. So that even within the tribe I was something of an outsider. Some even thought I was a Russian spy!

Often people first discover their sense of nationality when they are living in another country. One of the nuns at the Sacred Heart urged us to write a letter of protest to a senator about some issue—I no longer remember what it was. I was surprised, but I did write and was even more surprised when I received an answer. Whether or not he would take action on the issue, he actually answered me, which is something that never happens in Mexico. And as I began writing after my return to Mexico, I wrote out of my own reality—out of what I experienced and saw or was told or read. It is one thing to identify oneself as a citizen of a country and to love its landscape, its people, its arts and culture. It is quite another thing to assess the workings of its social and political structure—the degree of freedom and opportunity enjoyed by its people, its standard of education and quality of life. A Mexican peasant has virtually no chance of becoming anything else. The standard of education was low fifty years ago and, if anything, is even lower today. European workers, on the other hand, can travel the world—they can go to Egypt or China, wherever they please, certainly when they retire and even before that. They have a relatively big view of the world in this way. Mexican workers cannot travel the world and neither do they read, so their view is very narrow. Our current president, Enrique Peña Nieto, could not name three books he had read and finally was obliged to fall back on the Bible. Too bad he doesn't read the Mexican Constitution before going to bed. At least it would have something to do with his job!

There is an immense abyss between the very few who have money and the vast number who are poor—and there is scarce concern on the part of those who have for those who do not. The politicians can be numbered among those who have. So my being a Mexican writer and loving my country has come to find its expression in opening up this reality to other Mexicans and to the larger world, expressed through the voices of the least empowered—women, especially, and poor people of both genders.

INTERVIEWER

You have said that, in some sense, you were radicalized by the events of Tlatelolco— by the government's reaction to the quake and its responsibility for the structural weaknesses of the buildings that collapsed. What did it mean to you to be "radicalized," and what were you trying to achieve in the books you wrote about these events?

PONIATOWSKA

To respond to your last remark first, I don't think I have ever tried to "achieve" anything in my writing except to produce a good book. Which is to say, to follow Buffon's prescription of thinking, feeling, and expressing well, with clarity of mind, soul, and taste. I never followed a plan, I follow my instinct. There are times in the history of literature—I think of the England of Elizabeth or of eighteenth-century France—when, for some reason that has to do with the development of the language or ... I don't know what, it would have been difficult to write badly. That is less true now. So I work to pare down passages that are unnecessarily long and to eliminate sentences that I love but that call too much attention to themselves. These things are well known to all writers.

As for being radicalized, I may be guilty myself of having used that word. More accurately, nothing new was revealed to me by these events. One saw the evidence of corruption daily, but here it was, as Americans say, in your face—soldiers shooting and killing innocent people, mothers and children and unarmed students conducting a peaceful demonstration in an open space with no means of escape since the streets leading to it had been barred.

Beyond that, the events of Tlatelolco happened soon after the death of my younger brother, at the age of twenty-one. His death had nothing to do with those events, but, of course, had the effect of enabling me to grieve *with* the survivors and to feel, in a personal way, the terrible loss of young lives, full of promise. At the same time, if my own grief had entered too directly into the book, it would have weakened it. The events themselves and the voices of the people who experience them are more than enough.

INTERVIEWER

Of course there is judgment, implicit and explicit, in what you write, and yet not from within an ideology. You have made visible real people who were barely seen. Jesusa is a *person*, as are all the people who have spoken to you about their suffering. You have been much written about in academic circles, but I think they will have a hard time pigeonholing you.

PONIATOWSKA

Perhaps if I had to put myself in some category of that sort, I would call myself a reactionary Romantic!

INTERVIEWER

I have the sense you mean that somewhat tongue-in-cheek. Even so, what might you say about such a category?

PONIATOWSKA

That is not an easy question to answer because, as you say, I'm not in any sense an ideologue. My father's mother was an American, Elizabeth Sperry Crocker, and through her I am descended from Benjamin Franklin. Although Franklin spent almost a decade in Paris, he is the only person from this side of the Atlantic who might be styled a philosophe in the manner of Voltaire, and with almost the same prestige. The vision of democracy these Enlightenment figures had— so eloquently expressed, for example, by Jefferson, and so practically carried out by Franklin and, in his own way, by Stanisław—is perhaps what I have in mind by "reactionary Romantic." In this way, I can point to it, rather than define it.

INTERVIEWER

Have you felt yourself to be part of a community of writers and intellectuals in Mexico? Or, instead, as a person deeply engaged in her work who, despite friendships among such people, is otherwise solitary?

I am not sure that writers have ever constituted a community, although, when letters were the only means of communication, people—literary people, scientists, mathematicians—kept up international connections in what might

Protesting the murders of *La Jornada* correspondent Javier Valdez and other journalists, in Mexico City, 2017. "In Mexico, because of the suffering that is the result of centuries of corruption, there is a moral obligation to write of this. I could not ignore it."

be called a community of letters. I know and have known many Mexican writers whose friendship and work I have enjoyed and respected, but I cannot say that we constitute a community. Those early years at the Centro Mexicano de Escritores had a role in my inclusion in the world of Mexican letters. But I think, with significant exceptions, the content of my work was often more specifically related to the social problems of my country than to the work of others. Of them all, I felt closest to my dear friend Carlos Monsiváis, who, along with Carlos Fuentes, was perhaps the Mexican writer of my generation whom I felt most as a kindred spirit.

In the border states, walls are being built to keep immigrants from crossing. But what you have suggested is that Mexico is already a walled nation—its people cannot travel, cannot broaden their vision of the world, are the prisoners of mind-numbing telenovelas and newspapers that reveal nothing of the deeper truth. With colleagues, you founded *La Jornada*, a daily independent newspaper, to provide another voice. Yet you've looked back at your life and, despite its satisfactions, feel you have not done all that you should have. But what could any of us do to put this country, with its centuries-long history of corruption, on a different footing?

PONIATOWSKA

People seem heartened by the tapering off of the so-called War on Drugs, which killed in the range of a hundred and seventy-five thousand people, including many journalists. The industry includes not only drugs but gunrunning and human trafficking and could not have succeeded without government corruption. They also seem encouraged by the visit of President Obama.

INTERVIEWER

And are you encouraged by these things?

PONIATOWSKA

Perhaps it is part of being a "reactionary Romantic" that I do not lose hope in the face of repeated failures or the sense of an obligation to speak on behalf of people who suffer as the consequence of centuries of corruption. Some of this comes from my upbringing and later from a profound reawakening to the reality of my country that came with the events of the massacre at Tlatelolco. The question of being encouraged or discouraged by this or that event cannot be asked if one is to go on with a certain moral conviction. Although I know very little about Buddhism, I believe that this is what Buddhists refer to as "right understanding"—that is to say, acting out of compassion, informed by as much awareness as one can muster. The ultimate outcome of our actions cannot be known. But despite our limited awareness, I believe we must always act with compassion.

Two Poems by Alejandra Pizarnik

TO YOU

to you
the view
to me
the months
memory
armoire of glory
sullen salon of salt
you up high
announcement annulled
the arc the archaic
everything's weight
strangles
strange circle
love me
it's your play
I say
no one says
nothing says
the back of the curtain
makes love to the wind
I wait
until they finish up
living
without you
at dawn without you
I see myself naked
among the dross
that we toss
each to her place
to cry
to speak

an absence
to each her own absence
I've chosen
I've gone pure
I drank to see him again
at the bottom of your wine
your cry in vain

MEMORY NEAR OBLIVION

Memory near oblivion. Far death
the voice grinds and vibrates and trembles
the wind denies
the wind lies
the vain wind
the hand hides
the holy hand
the sent saint
the saint inseminated
by the wind that lies
I lie
I deny
I lie down
from gold and from grind
these demented hands are mine
my holy hands
inseminated by your shadow
I collapse
I touch myself
a flower's gesture
frail
cold
I offer myself awfully
abyss frost
I offer myself
you frighten me
I offer myself
I don't give a fuck

—Translated from the French by Patricio Ferrari and Forrest Gander

The Shape of the Mountain

—

ETEL ADNAN

CURATED BY
NICOLE RUDICK

Once things leave my files," Etel Adnan wrote to me, "I never know where they are, and don't think about them anymore, otherwise you lose your mind." Her method is sound: now ninety-three, she has made hundreds of works over seven decades and shows no signs of slowing. She made the painting on the cover of this issue in January, especially for *The Paris Review* (the pencil marks are hers, too). So numerous are her paintings, drawings, films, tapestries, ceramics, and murals that I imagine it must be impossible to see them all; so brisk and vital are they that I am always eager for more— and amazed by the beauty she discovers each time.

Adnan was born in Beirut in 1925. Her mother was from Smyrna, her father an Ottoman officer from Damascus; at home, they spoke Turkish and Greek, and she was educated in French. She studied philosophy at the Sorbonne and traveled from there to Berkeley and Harvard. It was the United States—California specifically—that made Adnan a painter. She took her first art class at Dominican College, north of San Francisco, where she was teaching the philosophy of art. When the war for Algerian independence began in 1954, she became hardened against the French language, in which she had been writing poetry. "Painting," she says, "opened to me a different way of expression. And as my Arabic was poor, in some moment, as a defiance, I happened to say, I will paint in Arabic!" The California landscape awakened her spiritual instincts and focused her gaze. While living near Mill Valley, she had daily views of Mount Tamalpais. "To observe its constant changes became my major preoccupation," she has written. "I even wrote a book in order to come to terms with it—but the experience overflowed my writing. I was addicted."

Adnan never left the mountain behind. It appears decade after decade in various guises: as monochromatic mounds, thin washes of color, accumulations of brushy strokes. Her landscapes, too, are variations on a theme—minimal fields of color describing anonymous grassy hills, alluvial plains, quiet oceans—but each color combination, each arrangement of forms evokes a new mood. In *Journey to Mount Tamalpais*, published in 1986, Adnan writes that the "pyramidal shape of the mountain reveals a perfect Intelligence within the universe. Sometimes its power to melt in mist reveals the infinite possibilities for matter to change its appearance." That mystical geometry extends to the cosmos, the busy orbiting of swift planets and the pendulous drift of the sun and moon—celestial bodies that both possess a physical reality and act as gateways to another place or dimension. "Voyager 2 has already travelled 2 billion miles," she writes in *Journey*. "We are well engaged into the outer frontiers. And further on, when we will go beyond the reaches of Space and Time, something else will open up, we will know what it means for the human species to become an Angel."

Color is essential to these transfigurations. When Adnan sees Tamalpais topped with snow, she muses that "white is the color of terror in this century: the great white mushroom, the white and radiating clouds, the White on White painting by Malevich, and that whiteness, most fearful, in the eyes of men." Color is energy, a visionary pathway linking the earth and the universe. In that space, she gathers prophesy and myth, Arab mystics and Soviet cosmonauts, Friedrich Nietzsche and Eleni Sikélianòs. In a gouache and ink painting made in the eighties, she encircles the names of writers and artists she admires in bubbles rising against a loose grid of color, like a cultural solar system.

This page: *Untitled (Mt. Tamalpais 1)*, ca. 1995–2000, oil on canvas, 14" x 18". Following spread: *East River Pollution, "From Laura's window," New York, April 79* (detail), 1979, crayon and pencil on paper, thirty pages, each 8" x 3⅓", max. extension 7' ⅘".

In 1965, Adnan wrote what she has called her first American poem, in response to the escalation of the Vietnam War. Composing in English was "an adventure ... a sport," she has said. "Sentences were like horses, opening space in front of them with their energies, and beautiful to ride." Three years later, she produced her first *leporello*, an accordion-fold book that extends several feet in length; her longest is more than seventeen feet. On some of these, she copied Arabic poetry calligraphically, using ink and watercolor, rendering the poems visually, as landscapes of verse. In others, drawings gallop from page to page, unfurling, literally, across time.

98 Adna

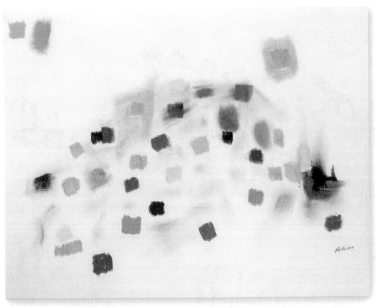

Opposite page: *Untitled*, 1998, watercolor on paper, 25 ⅗" x 19 ¾". This page, top: *Untitled*, ca. 1970,
pastel on paper, 9 ½" x 11 ⅘"; bottom: *La Montagne 7*, 2014, aquarelle and Chinese ink on paper, 20 ½" x 27 ⅗".
Following spread: *Kalimat* (detail), 2012, pencil and aquarelle on paper, sixty pages, each 10 ⅗" x 3 ½", max. extension 17' 8".

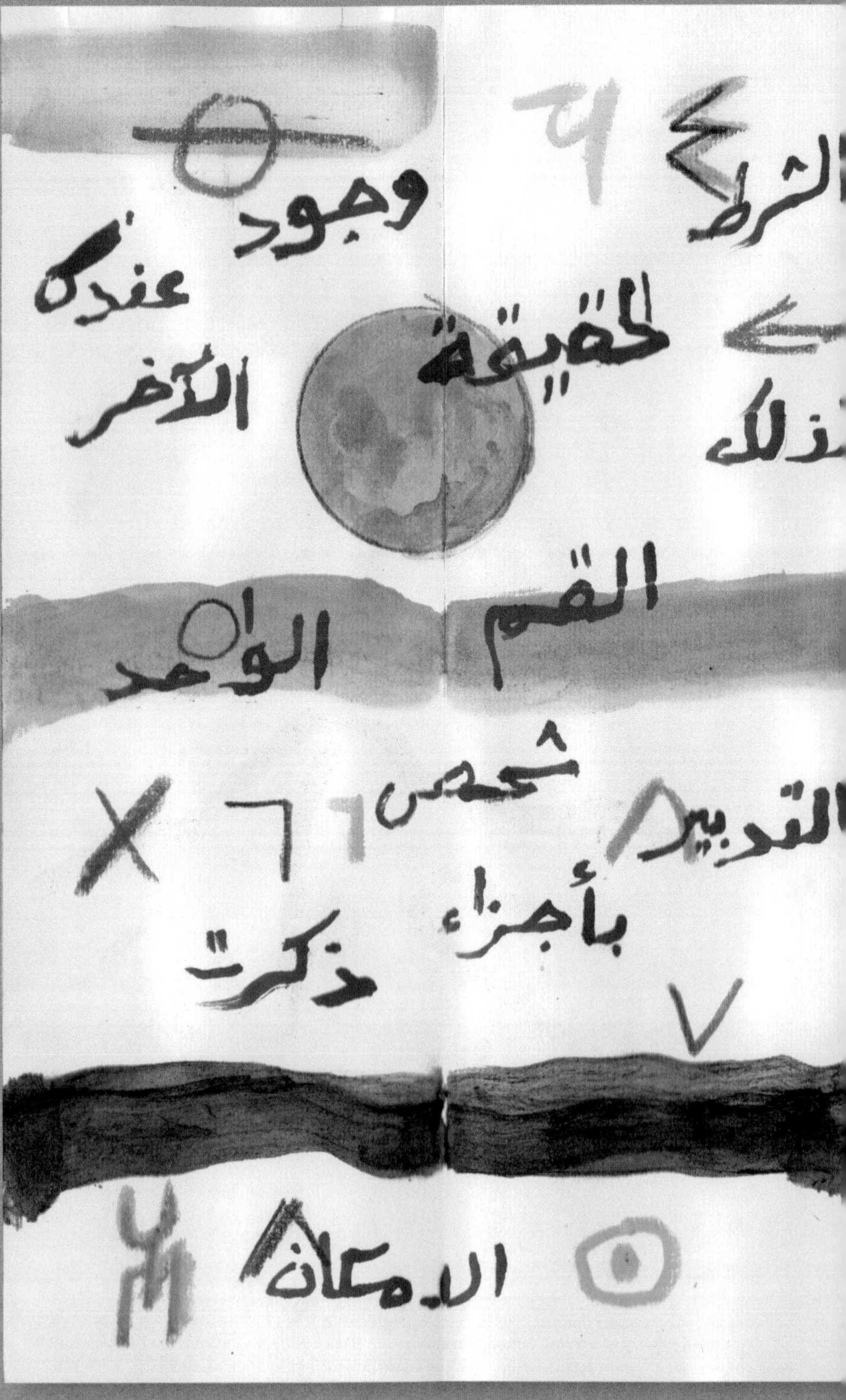

الشرط ◄ ٩

وجود ◯

عندك ذلك ◄ الحقيقة

الآخر

القمم الواحد

شمس ٦٦ X

التدوير ٨ بأجزاء ذكرت

٧

الإمكان ٣ ⊙

اللون ٨

البحر الخريف

الصيف الأ

٩

الجلد

الأم ١

السطح

الآب

المطبخ ٣

الملح

This page: *Paysage 1*, 2014, oil on canvas, 12⅗" x 16". Opposite page: *Le poids du monde 19*, 2016, oil on
canvas, 12⅓" x 9⅘". Following spread: *Untitled* (detail), 1989, watercolor on paper, 18" x 27".

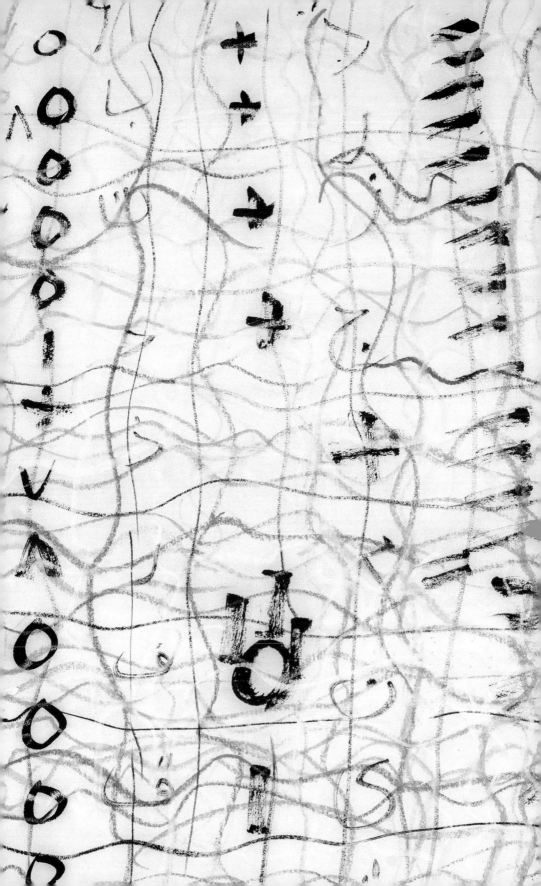

Opposite page: *Untitled*, ca. 1960s, watercolor on paper, 10" x 8".
This page: *Arizona*, 1964–65, oil on canvas, 30" x 28 ½".

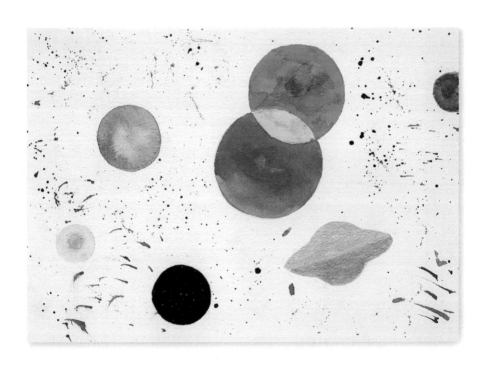

Opposite page: *Le poids du monde 17*, 2016, oil on canvas, 12 ⅓" x 9 ⅘". This page: *Untitled*, 1995,
watercolor on paper, 8 ⅓" x 11 ⅗". Following spread: *Untitled*, 1982–85, gouache and ink on paper, 19 ¾" x 25 ½".

Sappho Emily
Dickinson Francis
Villon Maurice Scève
Charles d'Orléans
Milosz Pouchkine
Mallarmé

the poets
of Compages the
poets of Africa the
poets of Guatemala
of Nicaragua
Maiakowski
Blok Akh-
matova

Racine Paul
Valéry Hart Crane
Whitman Kleist
Hölderlin Novalis
Pablo Neruda
Vallejo

Yevtuchenko
Thabo June
Jordan Sarah
Miles Saint John
Perse John of the
Cross Paul Éluard
René Char
Desnos

Cavafy Elity
Sekelianos
Ritsos Mahmoud
Darwiche Badr
Shaker al Sayyab
Jundi
Azzawi

Shakespeare
Virgil Lucretius
Michaux Antonin
Artaud Louise
Labé John Beecher
Enrique Bonaventura
Jorge Argueta
Flaxman Doo
pane

Kate Ryan
the poets of
Japan the poets
of China Ok-Koo
Kwang-John Lennon
Suhrawardi Abu
Ala al Maarri
Heinrich Heine

Fouad Gabriel
Nafah. Verlaine
Gerard de Nerval
Chawki Ibn al
Fared Rumi
Muhyeddin Ibn
Al-Arabi
Hafez

...diba
...ghlatti
...Arati Pushke
... Katerina
... David Vol-
...esta

Antonio Machado
Jorge Guillen TS
Eliott Ted Hughes
Tranströmer Paula
Gunn Allen
Yusef el Khal
Georges Sche'
hadeh

...trischman...
...nah Mennefee
...erico Garcia
...a Lautréamont
...dnan Baudelaire
...Bruno Gulli

Saâdi al
Niffari Al
Hallaj Pierre Jean
Jouve Michaux
American Indian
poets Yunus
Emre Hikmet
al Bayati

Al Mutanabbi
Allen Ginsberg
Shelley Yeats
Keats Robinson
Jeffers Rosmarie
Waldrop
Adonis

Rimbaud
Corbière
...ssoa
...ytieri
Noel
...rave
...chelri

Kamala Das
Gabriela Mistral
Amanda Berenguer
Ingrid Jonker Stella
Ngatho Abdel Latif
Laabi Leila Djabali
Hatspshapsut
Nsaïda wAïï
Attik

Genny Lim
Fowaz Turki
Mercedes Durand
Peter Jurgen Boock
André Breton Paul
Landry Silya
Yapita Laura
Manlio Argueta
Alixa

Enheduanna
Elizabeth Barrett
Browning Dylan
Thomas Zinaida
Z. Gippius Stein
E. Vakalo Barbara
Stampa D'Annun-
zio Michel
Couturier

E.A.

This page: *Untitled*, 2015, oil on canvas, 16⅛" x 13". Opposite page: *Untitled* (detail), 2014, oil on canvas, 12" x 9½". Following spread: *Untitled*, 1998, watercolor on paper, 19⅗" x 27½".

Adrian 98

Major Jackson

IN MEMORY OF DEREK ALTON WALCOTT

I

Island traffic slows to a halt
as screeching gulls reluctant
to lift heavenward
congregate like mourners in salt-
crusted kelp, as the repellent
news spreads to colder shores:

Sir Derek is no more.
Bandwidths, clogged by streaming
tributes, carry the pitch
of his voice, less so his lines, moored
as they are to a fisherman's who strains
in the Atlantic

then hearing, too, drops his rod, the reel
unspooling like memory till
his gaped mouth matches
the same look in his wicker creel,
that frozen shock, eyes marble
a different catch.

Pomme-Arac trees, sea grapes,
and laurels sway, wrecked having lost
one who heard their leaves'
rustic dialect as law, grasped
their bows as edicts from the first
garden that sowed faith—

and believe he did, astonished
at the bounty of light, like Adam,
over Castries, Cas-
en-Bas, Port of Spain, the solace
of drifting clouds, rains like hymns
then edens of grass,

ornate winds on high verandas
carrying spirits who survived
that vile sea crossing,
who floated up in his stanzas,
the same souls Achille saw alive,
the ocean their coffin—

faith, too, in sunsets, horizons
whose auric silhouettes divide
and spawn reflection,
which was his pen's work, devotion
twinned with delight, divining
like a church sexton.

Poetry is empty without
discipline, without piety,
he cautions somewhere,
even his lesser rhymes amount
to more than wrought praise but amplify
his poems as high prayer.

So as to earn their wings above,
pelicans move into tactical
formation then fly
low like jet fighters in honor of
him, nature's mouth, their aerial
salute and goodbye.

2

Derek, each journey we make,
whether Homeric or not,
follows the literal wake
of some other craft's launch,

meaning to sense the slightest
motions in unmoving waters
is half the apprentice's
training before he oars

out, careful to coast, break-
ing English's calm surface.
What you admired in Eakins
in conversation at some café

(New Orleans? Philly?) was
how his rower seemed to listen
to ripples on the Schuylkill as
much as to his breath, both silent

on his speaking canvas.
Gratitude made you intolerant
of the rudeness of the avant-
garde or any pronouncements

of the "new," for breathing is
legacy and one's rhythm,
though the blood's authentic
transcription, hems us

to ancestors like a pulse. This,
I fathom, is what you meant
when exalting the merits
of a fellow poet: *that man*

is at the center of language,
at the center of the song.
Yet a reader belongs to another age
and, likely to list our wrongs

more than the strict triumphs
of our verse, often retreats
like a vanished surf, spume
frothing on a barren beach.

The allure of an artist's works
these days is measured
by his ethics, thus our books,
scrubbed clean, rarely mention

the shadowless dark that settles
like an empire over a page. Your nib,
like the eye of a moon, flashed into sight
the source of Adam's barbaric cry.

3

Departed from paradise,
each *Nobody* a sacrifice,
debating whose lives matter
whereon a golden platter

our eyes roll dilated by hate
from Ferguson to Kuwait.
You, *maître*, gave in laughter
but also for the hereafter

an almost unbearable
truth: we are the terrible
history of warring births
destined for darkest earth.

So as cables of optic lights
bounce under oceans our white
pain, codified as they are
and fiber-layered in Kevlar,

we hear ourselves in you,
where "race" exiles us to
stand lost as single nations
awaiting your revelations.

A shirtless boy, brown as bark,
gallops alongshore, bareback
and free on a horse until he fades,
a shimmering, all that remains.

Justice

RACHEL CUSK

I had been told that the interviewer was waiting for me outside in the hotel garden. The muffled oceanic roar of traffic rose steadily from the nearby road. She was sitting alone on a bench amid the raw planted beds and network of gravel paths, gazing down the hill toward the city where the snaking dark shape of the river wound through the old town, trapped by the intricate architecture clamped to its sides. The blackened spikes of the cathedral could be seen jutting above the rooftops.

She had come directly from the train station on foot, she said, since in this city to go anywhere by car was effectively a diversion from one's aims. The postwar road system had been built, apparently, without thought for the notion of traveling between two points. The giant freeways circled the city without penetrating it, she said: to get anywhere, you had to go everywhere; the roads were permanently jammed while lacking the logic of a common destination. But it was a perfectly pleasant short walk through the center. She stood up to shake my hand.

"Actually," she said, "we've met before."

I know, I said, and her huge eyes lit up for a second in her gaunt face.

"I wasn't sure you'd remember," she said.

It had been more than ten years ago, yet the encounter had stayed with me, I said. She had described her home and her life in a way that had often returned to me during those years and that I could still clearly recall. Her description of the town where she lived—a place I had never been to, though I knew it wasn't far from here—and of its beauty had been particularly tenacious: it had often, as I said, returned to my mind, to the extent that I had wondered why it did. The reason, I thought, was that this description had a finality to it that I couldn't imagine ever attaining in my own circumstances. She had talked about the placid neighborhood where she had her home with her husband and children, with its cobbled streets too narrow for cars to pass down, so that nearly everyone traveled by bicycle, and where the tall, slender-gabled houses were set back behind railings from the silent waterways on whose banks great trees stood, holding out their heavy arms so that they made plunging green reflections in the stillness below, like mirrored mountains. Through the windows you could hear the sounds of footsteps on the cobbles below and the hiss and whir of bicycles passing in their shoals and drifts; and most of all you could hear the bells that rang unendingly from the town's many churches, striking not just the hours but the quarter and half hours, so that each segment of time became a seed of silence that then blossomed, filling the air with what almost seemed a kind of self-description. The conversation of these bells, held back and forth across the rooftops, was continued night and day: its cadences of observation and agreement, its passages of debate, its longer narratives—at Matins and Evensong, for instance, and most of all on Sundays, the repeating summons building and building until it was followed at last by the joyous, deafening exposition—comforted her, she had said, as the sound of her parents' lifelong conversation had comforted her in her childhood, the rise and fall of their voices always there in the next room, discussing and observing and noting each thing that happened, as though they were making an inventory of the whole world. The quality of the town's silence, she had said, was something she only really noticed when she went elsewhere, to places where the air was filled with the drone of traffic and of music blaring out of restaurants and shops and the cacophony from the endless construction sites where buildings were forever being torn down and then put up again. She would come home to a silence that at those times felt so refreshing it was like swimming in cool water, and she would, for a period, be aware of how the bells, far from disturbing the silence, were in fact defending it.

Her description of her life had struck me, I said to her now, as that of a life lived inside the mechanism of time, and whether or not it was a life everyone would have found desirable, it had seemed at the very least to lack a quality that drove other people's lives into extremity, whether of pleasure or of pain.

She lifted her elegant eyebrows, her head tilted to one side.

That quality, I said, could almost be called suspense, and it seemed to me to be generated by the belief that our lives were governed by mystery, when in fact that mystery was merely the extent of our self-deception over the fact of our own mortality. I had often thought of her, I said, in the years since we had last met, and those thoughts had tended to occur when I myself had been driven into extremity by the suspicion that some knowledge was being withheld from me whose revelation would make everything clear. She had talked, I said, about her husband and two sons and about the simple, regulated life they lived, a life that involved little change and hence little waste, and the fact that in certain details her life had mirrored my own while in no way resembling it had often led me to see my situation in the most unflattering light. I had broken that mirror, I said, without knowing whether I had done so as an act of violence or simply by mistake. Suffering had always appeared to me as an opportunity, I said, and I wasn't sure I would ever discover whether this was true and, if so, why it was, because so far I had failed to understand what it might be an opportunity for. All I knew was that it carried a kind of honor, if you survived it, and left you in a relationship to the truth that seemed closer, but that in fact might have been identical to the truthfulness of staying in one place.

The interviewer sat with her light, bony limbs gracefully crossed and an expression of increasing severity on her face, which was deeply lined and shadowed, particularly beneath the eyes, where the skin almost looked bruised. Her head was bent and drooped on her long, thin neck like the head of a dark flower while she listened.

"I admit," she said finally, "that I took pleasure in telling you about my life and in making you feel envious of me. I was proud of it. I remember thinking, Yes, I've avoided making a mess of things, and it seemed to me that it was through hard work and self-control that I had, rather than luck. But it was important not to look as if I was boasting. It always felt then as if I had a secret," she said, "and it would have ruined things if I had let it out. When I used to look at my husband, I knew that he had the same secret, and I knew that he would never tell it either because it was something we shared, like actors secretly share the knowledge that they're acting, which if they openly admitted to doing so would ruin the scene. Actors need an audience," she said, "and so did we, because part of the pleasure was showing our secret without telling it."

Over the years, they had watched their contemporaries fall at one hurdle or another, and they had even tried to help in these emergencies, which only increased their feeling of superiority. At around the time she met me, she went on, she had a good friend at home who was going through a terrible divorce and who spent a lot of time at their house getting support and advice. The two families had been close and had spent many evenings and weekends and holidays in one another's company, but now a completely different reality was revealed. Every day this friend would appear with some new story of horror: the husband had arrived with a van and taken all the furniture when she wasn't there, or he had left the children alone all weekend when it was his turn to have them; then that he was forcing her to sell the home where they'd lived all their lives and going around to all their friends saying the most awful things about her and poisoning their minds against her. She would sit at our kitchen table, the interviewer said, pouring out these stories in utter shock and dismay, and my husband and I would listen and try to comfort her. But at the same time, it gave us a kind of pleasure to watch her, though we would never, ever have admitted it to each other, because the pleasure was part of our unspoken secret.

"The fact was," the interviewer went on, "that my husband and I had once envied this woman and the man she was married to, whose life at one time had seemed in numerous ways superior to our own. They were very lively and adventurous people," she said, "and they were always setting off with their children on exotic travels, and they also had very good taste, so that their home was full of beautiful, unusual objects, as well as the evidence of their creativity and love of high culture. They painted and played musical instruments and read a tremendous number of books, and as a family they behaved in ways that always seemed more free-spirited and fun than our own family activities managed to be. It was the only time—when we were with them," she said—"that I became dissatisfied with our life and with our characters and our children's characters. I envied them, because they seemed to have more than we had, and I couldn't see what they had done to deserve it."

In short, she had been jealous of this friend, who was very attractive and who nevertheless constantly complained about her lot, about the injustices of motherhood or the indignity of the domestic work involved in bringing up a family. Yet the one thing she never complained about was her husband, and perhaps for this reason the husband became the thing the interviewer envied her for most of all, to the extent that he almost succeeded in making her own husband look inadequate to her. He was bigger and more handsome than her husband, extremely charming and sociable, and he possessed a formidable range of physical and intellectual talents, winning every game he played and always knowing more than anyone else on any subject. In addition, he was very domesticated and appeared to be the ideal father, spending all his time gardening and cooking with the children and taking them on camping and sailing trips. Most of all, he was sympathetic to his wife's complaining, and was always egging her on to become more and more indignant about the travails and oppressions of womanhood, which he himself did so much to relieve her of.

"My own husband," she said, "was physically unconfident and also spent so much time in his law office that he missed out on many of our family routines, and these failures—which were the cause of private feelings of resentment and anger for me—I energetically concealed, boasting instead about his importance and how hard he worked, to the extent that I almost succeeded in denying those feelings to myself. Only when we were with this other couple did the truth threaten to become apparent, and I wondered sometimes whether my husband had ever guessed my thoughts or might even have privately suspected me of being in love with this other man. But if it was love," the interviewer said, "then it was of the kind the Bible calls covetousness, and my friend's husband enjoyed nothing more than being coveted. Never have I met a man so dedicated to maintaining appearances," she said, "to the extent that I came to see something almost female in him, despite the manliness of his persona. I felt a great kinship with him, and never more than when I was boasting about my husband's slavish dedication to his work, and he was likewise taking his wife's part and describing some undignified aspect of her life as a woman. In a way, we recognized one another: we liked one another as a way of liking ourselves, although of course, nothing was ever said, because then the picture we had made of our lives would have been completely ruined. My friend once told me," she went on, "that her mother had said to her that she didn't deserve her husband. And at the time," the interviewer said, "I privately agreed, but in the divorce those words took on an entirely opposite meaning."

With each fresh story she heard at the kitchen table, she said, she was forced to wonder more and more about the character of this man, which she had at one time found so appealing and even now, with the evidence before her, had trouble condemning. And she would look at her own husband sitting patiently and kindly while their friend talked, though he was exhausted from work and hadn't even had time to change out of his suit, and she would feel astonished anew at her good sense in choosing him. The more terrible things their friend said about the other man, the more she hoped no one had noticed how much she had liked him, to the extent that she began to criticize him harshly, even though she still secretly thought the friend might be exaggerating the things he had done. And her husband, she noticed, was unusually critical of him, too, so that she began to see that he had actually hated him all along.

"It started to seem," she said, "as if between us we had somehow brought the destruction of their family life about, as if my secret love and his secret hate had conspired to destroy the object of their disagreement. Each night after our friend had gone home we would sit and talk quietly about her situation, and it felt like we were writing a story together," she said, "where things that never happened in reality were allowed to happen and justice could be done, and it all seemed to be coming from inside our own heads, except that it was also happening in actuality. We became closer than we had been in a while. It was a good time in our marriage," she said, with a bitter smile. "It was as if all the things we had envied in that other marriage had been released and bequeathed to us."

She turned her head, still smiling, and looked down the hill toward the city, where cars were moving in swarms along the roads beside the river. The distinctive shape of her nose, which from the front slightly marred her fine-featured face, in profile attained beauty: it was upturned and snub-ended and had a deep V in its bridge, as though someone had drawn it with a certain license, to make a point about the relationship between destiny and form.

I said that while her story suggested that human lives could be governed by the laws of narrative, and all the notions of retribution and justice that narrative lays claim to, it was, in fact, merely her interpretation of events that created that illusion. The couple's divorce, in other words, had nothing to do with her secret envy of them and her desire for their downfall: it was her own capacity for storytelling—which, as I had already told her, had affected me all those years ago—that made her see her own hand in what happened around her. Yet the suspicion that her own desires were shaping the lives of other people, and even causing them to suffer, did not seem to lead her to feel guilt. It was an interesting idea, I said, that the narrative impulse might spring from the desire to avoid guilt, rather than from the impulse—as was generally assumed—to connect things together in a meaningful way; that it was a strategy calculated, in other words, to disburden ourselves of responsibility.

"But you believed my story all those years ago," she said, "despite the fact that I didn't expect you to and that probably I only wanted to make my life seem enviable so that I could accept it myself. My whole career," she said, "has involved interviewing women—politicians, feminists, artists—who have made their female experience public and who are willing to be honest about one aspect of it or another. It has been up to me to represent their honesty," she said, "while at the same time being far too timid to live life in the way they do, according to feminist ideals and political principles. It was easier to think," she said, "that my own way of life involved its own courage, the courage of consistency. And I did come to revel in the difficulties such women experienced, while at the same time appearing to sympathize with them.

"As a child," she said, "I used to see my sister, who was two years older than me, take the brunt of whatever came, while I watched it all from the safety of my mother's lap. And every time she went wrong or made a mistake, I made a note to myself not to do the same thing when it was my turn. There were often terrible arguments," she said, "between my sister and my parents, and I profited from them simply by not being the cause of them, so that when it came to these interviews, I found I was in a familiar position. I seemed to profit," she said, "from the mere fact of not being these public women, while they were in a sense fighting my cause, just as my sister had fought my cause by demanding certain freedoms that I was then easily granted when I reached the same age. I wondered whether one day I might have to pay for this privilege, and, if so, whether the reckoning might come in the form of female children, and each time I was pregnant, I hoped so ardently for a boy that it seemed impossible that my wish would be granted. Yet each time, it was," she said, "and I watched my sister struggle with her daughters as I had always watched her struggle with everything, with the satisfaction of knowing that by watching closely enough I had avoided her mistakes. Perhaps for that reason," she said, "it was almost unbearable to me when my sister made a success of something. Despite the fact that I loved her, I couldn't tolerate the spectacle of her triumph.

"The friend that I told you about earlier," she said, "was in fact my sister, and it did seem to me that her divorce and the destruction of her family was the thing I had been waiting for all my life. In the years that followed," she said, "I would sometimes look at her daughters and I would almost hate them for the damage and suffering that showed in their faces, because the sight of these damaged children reminded me that it was not, after all, a game anymore, the old simple game where I profited by watching, as it were, from the safety of my mother's lap. My own sons continued to live normal lives, full of security and routine, while my sister's house was racked by the most terrible troubles, troubles she continued to be honest about, to the point where I told her I thought she was damaging the children even more by not putting up a pretense for them. In the end, I became reluctant to expose my own children to it, because I worried they would find the sight of such violent emotion disturbing, and so I stopped inviting them to our house and to come on holiday with us, as I had regularly done up until then.

"It was at that point," she said, "when I took my eyes off my sister's household, that things began to change for her. I noticed, in the communications I still had with my sister, that she sounded calmer and more optimistic; I began to hear stories of her daughters' small successes and improvements. One day," she said, "I was on my bicycle and it began suddenly to pour with rain. For once I had come out without my waterproof, and looking for somewhere to shelter, I realized I was close to my sister's house. It was early in the morning and I knew she would be at home, so I pedaled through the rain to her front door and I rang the bell. I was completely bedraggled and soaking wet, as well as wearing my oldest clothes, and it didn't even occur to me that someone other than my sister might open the door. To my surprise, it was a man who opened it, a good-looking man who immediately stepped back to let me in and who took my wet things and offered me a towel to dry my hair with. I knew," she said, "the instant I laid eyes on him, that this was my sister's new partner, and that he was a far better man than the husband I had once envied her for, and it was indeed the case that he represented a change in her fortunes and in her daughters' fortunes, too. I realized," she said, "that she was happy for the first time in her life, and I realized, too, that she would never have known this happiness had she not gone through the unhappiness that preceded it, in precisely the way that she did. She had once said that her former husband's cold and selfish character, which none of us—she least of all—had really perceived, had been like a kind of cancer: invisible, it had lain within her life for years, making her more and more uncomfortable without her knowing what it was, until she had been driven by pain to open everything up and tear it out. It was then that our mother's cruel words—that my sister hadn't deserved her husband—came back to me with their altered meaning. At the time, it had seemed inexplicable to us all that my sister would leave such a husband, driving him into acts of whose callousness she was clearly the catalyst and doing irreparable harm to her children, but she now told a different story: his incipient callousness was the thing from which she felt duty bound to save her children, despite the fact that at the time she couldn't really prove that it was there. My sister told me," she said, "that she and her husband were once having a discussion about the former GDR and the awful ways in which people betrayed one another under the regime of the Stasi, and she had made the point that none of us truly knows the extent of our own courage or cowardice, because in these times, those qualities are rarely tested. He had disagreed, very strangely: he said that under those same circumstances he knew he would be among the first to sell out his neighbor. That, my sister said, was the first clear glimpse she had had of the stranger inside the man she lived with, though there were many other incidents, obviously, during the course of their marriage that might have told her who he really was, had he not succeeded in persuading her that she had either dreamt them or made them up.

"My sister's daughters now went from strength to strength, and in the public exams they far outshone my own children, who nonetheless did well enough. My sons were pleasant and stable; they had identified career paths for themselves—one in engineering, the other in computer software—and as they prepared to leave school and go out into the world, I felt confident they would make responsible citizens. My husband and I, in other words, had done our duty, and it was now that I considered taking some of those feminist principles I had distributed far and wide and using them for myself. The truth was that I had long wondered what might lie outside the circumscribed world of my marriage, and what freedoms and pleasures might be waiting for me there: it seemed to me that I had behaved honorably toward my family and my community, and that this was a moment in which I could, as it were, resign without causing anger or hurt and get away under cover of darkness. And a part of me believed that I was owed this reward for those years of self-control and self-sacrifice, but another part merely wanted to win the game once and for all; to show a woman like my sister that it was possible to gain freedom and self-knowledge without having to smash up the whole world in public in the process.

"I imagined traveling," she said, "to India and Thailand, alone with a simple knapsack, moving lightly and swiftly after all the years of being weighed down; I imagined sunsets and rivers, and mountaintops visible on calm evenings. I imagined my husband at home in our house beside the canal, with our sons and his hobbies and his friends, and it seemed to me he might also be relieved," she said, "because over the two decades of our marriage, our male and female qualities had become blunted on one another. We lived together like sheep, grazing side by side, huddled next to one another in sleep, habituated and unthinking. I considered that there might be other men," she said, "and indeed for a long time other men had been appearing in my dreams, which otherwise were full of familiar people and familiar situations and anxieties. But these men who appeared were always strangers, based on no one I had ever known or met, and yet they recognized me with a special tenderness and desire, and I would recognize them, too, recognize in their faces something I felt I had once known but had forgotten or never found, and which I only remembered now, in the dream state. Of course, I could never tell anyone about these dreams, from which I woke feeling the most unbearable, exquisite happiness that quickly grew cold in the dawn light of our room and became disappointment. I have always been impatient with people who talk about their dreams," she said, "but I had a powerful desire to tell someone about these dreams of mine. Yet the only person I could think of to tell," she said, "was the man in the dream himself.

"At around this time," she went on, "my husband began to change in ways that were so small they were impossible to identify and at the same time impossible to ignore. It was almost as if he had become a copy or forgery of himself, someone otherwise identical who nonetheless lacked the authentic quality of the original. And indeed whenever I asked him what was wrong, he would always say the same thing, which was that he wasn't feeling quite himself. I asked our sons if they had noticed anything, and for a long time they denied it, but one evening, after the three of them had gone together to a football match—something they did regularly—they admitted that I was right and that he was somehow different. Again, it was impossible to say what the difference was, since he looked and behaved as normal. But he wasn't really there, they said, and it occurred to me that this quality of absence might signify that he was having an affair. And indeed one evening in the kitchen shortly afterward he suddenly said, very somberly, that he had some news for me. In that moment," she said, "I felt our whole life cleave apart, as though someone had cut it open with a great bright blade; I almost felt I could see the sky and the open air through the ceiling of our kitchen and feel the wind and rain coming through the walls. I had watched other couples separate," she said, "and it was usually like the separation of Siamese twins, a long drawn-out agony that in the end makes two incomplete and sorrowing people out of what was one. But this was so swift and sudden," she said, "a mere slicing of the rope that tethered us, that it felt almost painless. My husband was not having an affair, however," she said, tilting her head back toward the dull, gray sky and blinking her eyes several times. "What he had to tell me was not that our life together was over and that I was free, but that he was ill," she said, "an illness, moreover, that would not hasten his death but would instead blight every aspect of the life that remained to him. We had been married for twenty years," she said, "and he could easily live twenty more, the doctors had told him, each day losing some facet of his autonomy and potency, a reverse kind of evolution that would require him to pay back every single thing he had taken from life. And I, too, would have to pay," she said, "because the one thing that was forbidden to me was to desert him in his time of need, despite the fact that I no longer loved him and perhaps had never really loved him, and that, equally, he might not have ever loved me either. This would be the last secret we had to keep," she said, "and the most important one, because if this secret got out, all the others would, too, and the whole picture of life and of our children's lives we had made would be destroyed.

"My sister's new partner," she went on after a while, "has a house on one of the islands, the most beautiful island of them all. My husband and I had often fantasized about owning a property there, despite the fact that we could not have afforded even the smallest cowshed in that place. But it would have made our family complete, we felt, and it was something we always wanted that nonetheless remained outside our grasp. I have seen photographs of her partner's house," she said, "which is a spectacular place right by the water, and her children are sometimes in the photographs, and even though I know them well, they look like happy strangers. But I have never been to that house," she said, "and I will never go, despite the fact that my sister increasingly spends all her time there and even manages to complain about certain aspects of it, so that I have wondered whether one day she will reject it, as she has rejected nearly everything else she's been given. I no longer know what goes on inside my sister's head," she said, "because she no longer tells me, and it is this fact—that her life now has a secret of its own—that proves to me she will, after all, hold on to what she has. I sense that she would like never to see me again, and perhaps even never to see anyone. She has come to the end of her journey, a journey I have spent my whole life watching her make, and she has found what she wanted, despite my watching her with the greatest ambivalence. The effect has been to make her disappear from my view, as though I have forfeited my right to be able to see her. And I can't get over the feeling," she said, "that all of it was stolen from me."

She was silent for a while, her chin lifted and her eyes half closed. A bird landed inquiringly at her feet on the gravel path and sprang away again unnoticed.

"Now and again," she continued presently, "I have met people who have freed themselves from their family relationships. Yet there often seems to be a kind of emptiness in that freedom, as though in order to dispense with their relatives they had to dispense with a part of themselves. Like the man trapped in the glacier who cut off his own arm," she said, with a faint smile. "I don't intend to do that. My arm occasionally hurts me, but I see it as my duty to keep it. The other day," she said, "I met her first husband in the street. He was walking along holding a briefcase and wearing a suit, and I was surprised because this businessman's attire was something I had never associated with him: he had always been a bohemian, an artistic kind of person, and the fact that he would never stoop to working in an office—even if it meant his family was hard up—and condescended to the people who did, was one of the things that I guessed had riled my husband about him. My sister had earned the money in their household, and had even claimed—as a matter of feminist principle—to be glad that she did, but after their divorce, I suppose he had eventually had to fend for himself. In fact, I had privately admired his contempt for conventional men, and indeed I secretly shared it, so it was a surprise to me, as I say, to see him apparently dressed as one. We approached each other in the street and our eyes met, and I felt my old fondness for him spring up, in spite of everything that had happened. When we drew close enough I opened my mouth to speak, and only then did I see the expression of utter hatred on his face, so that for a moment I thought he might actually be about to spit at me. Instead, as he passed me, he hissed. It was a sound," she said, "such as an animal would make, and I was so shocked that I simply stood there in the street for a long time after he had walked away. The bells began to ring," she said, "and at the same time it started to rain, and I stood with my eyes fixed on the pavement, where the water was beginning to gather and to show the buildings and the trees and the people upside down in reflection. The bells rang and rang," she said, "and it must have been some special occasion, because I didn't think I had ever heard them ring for so long, to the point where I believed they would never stop. The melody they played got wilder and wilder and more and more nonsensical. But for as long as they rang," she said, "I was unable to move, and so I stood there with the water running down my hair and over my face and my clothes, watching the whole world gradually transfer itself into the mirror at my feet."

She fell silent, her mouth stretched in a strange grimace, her huge eyes unblinking, and the declivity of her nose a well of shadow in the changing light of the garden.

"You asked me earlier," she said to me, "whether I believed that justice was merely a personal illusion. I don't have the answer to that," she said, "but I know that it is to be feared, feared in every part of you, even as it fells your enemies and crowns you the winner."

Then, without saying anything more, she began to put her things in her bag with light, quick movements and turned to me with her hand outstretched. I took it and felt the surprising smoothness and warmth of her skin.

"I think I have everything I need," she said. "In fact, I looked up all the details before I came. It's what we journalists do nowadays," she said. "One day they'll probably replace us with a computer program. I read that you got married again," she added. "I admit that it surprised me. But don't worry, I won't be focusing on the personal elements. What matters is that it's a long, important piece. If I can get it done by the morning," she said, looking at her watch, "they may even put it in the afternoon edition."

Ange Mlinko

SLEEPWALKING IN VENICE

> Two kinds of imagination: the strong, the promiscuous.
> —Leopardi

Calle Rombiasio

Watching a boneless nymph's
half-hearted resurrection
from a spout in the pavement
over and over; catching a glimpse
of the source of my exhaustion,
as if my gaze all this time had lent

muscular support to her effort…
She wasn't at all as mischievous
as her sisters, who seeped up
through the flagstones of the court,
serving the blue basilica to us
repurposed as a teacup.

Nor was she as splenetic as
the poltergeist in the moka pot,
seething liquid from every fissure,
then exploding on its ring of gas.
If it seemed that water was fraught
with divinities under pressure,

maybe I was going mad myself,
just a little, in this hall of mirrors.
So much glass my eyes glazed over,
and green waves laminating a shelf

where recto sits, and verso appears
in blinding dazzle seeking cover.

Such a surplus of marble that
even in the apartment I occupied
(no palazzo), the stairs luminesced;
if, as Michelangelo had thought,
therein lurked an angel, it was mortified
under the tread of a houseguest.

But when I reached the door,
sprung the lock, climbed the last
spiral flight in thin air,
it was to a wheelhouse (more
or less) of a vessel held fast
to its view of the *sestiere*;

and I was alone with the seagulls,
listening to the creaking ropes
of dinghies below, whose sway
I felt—impossibly—in lulls
unaddressed as sails, or hopes:
tethered to my getaway.

San Marco

Morning glory folded in the scrolls
of columns dissolved their claims
to mass in a bisque-blue apparition;
dusk would blur the ink on rolls
recording their angelic names:
Fra Lippo Lapis, Azure-Titian . . .
like the boaters with their poles,
and not unlike the playground games

where you sidestep the cracks,
or leapfrog stepping-stones,
I tested substantiality bit by bit
with my whole body. Bones
of the duomo melt; how stacks
my hazy realness against it?

Scala d'Oro

I climbed the Golden Staircase.
Hadn't meant to. Who sightsees
council chambers? . . . Blasé
toward doge, lawyer, and delegate,
the scoop of whispering galleries,
I was arrested by the gilded vault
where images of Venus and her cult
were preamble to affairs of state.

Head tipped back, hand gripping rail . . .
I was bowled over by the hubris.
Reached the antechamber reeling
at what hung in the balance: pale
throats bared, a puff piece
for the ages floating on the ceiling.

Antechamber, Main Hall

It struck me that there'd been a fire
in these rooms, if not a brawl.
More *scuro* than *chiaro* in the employ
of the magistrates, choirs
of angels boiled up to forestall
their double-dealings with trompe l'oeil.

Sooty gold-and-black marble conspires
to churn an atmosphere of upheaval . . .

Yes, this place was unwholesome.
I made out Hera gifting a peacock
to the republic. Her crowded bower
jostled, unanchored the gaze from
any mooring, put the whole baroque
in service to the reigning power.

Compass Room

"Imagine me as a three-dimensional chessboard
on which several dozen games are being played
around the clock, with multiple figures
whose functions take some up and down the board,
unconstrained by distances; others are confined to diagonals;
and some are either on foot or afloat but never both,
who rest in velvet-lined beds after harlequin day,
a moonlit sapphire set in windows nightly . . .

"A room sighs when a door is opened, then closed.
I have hoarded all the thieves, swindlers, and traitors
in my iron stanzas like a bank vault on the understanding
that a productive interest grows in the smallest cell;
that iniquity builds under pressure, from a principal;
that to someone powerful somewhere this is valuable."

Piazzetta

Canal steps troubled by centuries
and off-the-shoulder things
that scandalize the sanctuaries
lead, among the stony echoings,

to wisdom like: *Never send an email*
when you're angry—and never
make a promise when you're happy. (Male
faces grinned.) *We should endeavor,*

one girl submitted, *to take a grain of salt*
with the outburst, the promise made in bed…
We should be trained to doubt; the default
will always be ardor. The cafés fed
their chatter into a cochlear gestalt,
a labyrinthine ear with no thread.

Vaporetto

No bellboys, no bellboys, I thought,
bumping the suitcase on each step,
not like Aschenbach had (what had I brought?
my hand squeezed bloodless by the strap).
And having failed to tip and fall,
I gave a last heave, and pushed the thing…
it snapped open like an arsenal
of folded silks (for parachute landing

in the dark, with flare)… Meanwhile
the bell buoys in the lagoon recorded data
regarding tides, temperature, salinity,
the migratory sands … and if a regatta
glanced off a satellite into infinity,
it hung like a chandelier in time's exile.

Envoi

She turned her ankle playing tennis
ten days before she was to go

on her first, lamentably shelved,
trip to Venice. How then is
she so long and so slow
to make amends to herself?...

Stepping back through the looking glass,
I'd tell my friends about the time
I made reservations for Venice,
then had to call them off, seeing as
I couldn't negotiate its sublime
on crutches, after a bout of tennis

on an uneven Moroccan clay court
put my right ankle in a cast.
The rhyme surely made an imprecation,
a sort of curse-cum-tort,
as well as the fact that, in contrast
to the sport, Venice is a game for one.

The stamp of the real authenticates
imagination's passport, I thought.
Yet as the train drew me backward
across the lagoon (whose cognates
include *lacuna*, of course), I fought
the cold, green voice that declared

It was as though she'd never been.
Yes? *Or it's that she went alone...*
and saw myself reflected nowhere,
deprived of some ... vitamin...
like a vampire feeling her bones
that can't find herself in a mirror...

But did she (a funny thing to ask)
sleep deeply, as I see she dreamed well?
I know mon ange—*her elaborate schemes;*

and in the city of the erotic masque,
her blindfolds and foam plugs are farcical;
bat-spread blackout curtains figure in regimes

where a plan of action or program
to lose consciousness is no paradox.
Refrigeration, wrapped in a duvet, is ideal…
The light doze ends at 1 A.M.—
an existential cry from the clocks,
the gulling of a campanile.

the — man in all
black christ rendom
Those who have
bowed their
knees to
Baal,

Citivas Dei
antipodes
dissisibily

all the scourge
we carried in our
orbits

a man too sophisticated
for sanity.

he should not pray
himself but the others who
depended upon him being at his
best. Lieing awake,

2.

By the cooler,
a dented jar
checked with
shades. Turned.

Tried desith to sleep, knowing

Hours after his visitor left, he ~~lia awake in the~~
he looked back on his life and saw only a
~~darkness, tossing and turning, staining his rumpled bedsheets~~
gauntlet of work, even more difficult exercises in giving. He'd kicked his bedcovers off to the floor,
~~with sweat, scratching mosquito bites,~~ fatigued but unable to
and lie on his back in Tael blue pajamas with gold piping on the placket and around the neck,
~~sleep, though he futilely tried counting backwards from one~~
hoping if he was motionless sleep might come. But his
squited
~~hundred and lie flat on his back. His~~ mind churned on. ~~He stared~~
in
at the ceiling where he saw, ~~not the~~ broken plaster, or water
The face of Joanne had shaken certainly
~~marks, but instead~~ the man who ~~challenged~~ his ~~faith~~ that all were
wonderstill echoed in the lowest coils of his ears.
equal in the eyes of the Lord. ~~The moment was burned into the~~
Words hurling them
~~emulsion of his memory.~~ Smith had almost hissed, ~~the words split~~
at them like stones open his
~~them out so suddenly~~ and with such hurt, that he, about to ~~recite~~
mouth in a grandile, opening one of apothegms
~~for one of his sermons,~~ offering his standard ~~explanations~~ for
suffering, stopped as if he'd been slapped. All his explanations
were suspended, bracketed, and shimmering in their place was the
ineluctable
~~incontestable~~ presence of this man who could have been his
brother were it not for the fact that he appeared to be damned.
Or fallen.
~~Truly damned.~~ Yes, he could admit it now: Their physical likeness
frightened him. What were the chances of encountering a double
for oneself? ~~One the Lord despised.~~ Yet there he'd been, as if
his own father had spit them out one, two. Like that. ~~But how~~
~~back he'd seemed!~~ Nevertheless, he ~~had felt his visitor's~~
~~intelligence. There was about him an air of arrogant pride and~~

and Despite his misfortunes, he was intelligent, spirited, solitary,
divided and above all else so very much in need

How strange it always was; someone
standing before him, invisible, someone
that even worse, was more invisible than they
need, or, he
because they could have
them.

the invisible
serves most
from others
simply.

And what had he wanted? A joke as his clergy?!
My God, didn't he have enough trouble already?

The Art of Fiction No. 239

CHARLES JOHNSON

Charles Johnson's historical slave narrative, *Middle Passage*, winner of the National Book Award for Fiction in 1990, defies genre. Framed in part as a nautical epic with echoes of Conrad and Melville, there is also a Swiftian current running through it, with variations on the Sinbad stories and Vedic myths. Such transgressions of form suffuse Johnson's fiction. His four novels and three story collections incorporate fairy tale, parable, conversion narrative, picaresque, bildungsroman, and more. Johnson's balance of playfulness and philosophical rigor also energizes his screenplays for television and film, two collections of humor writing, and several volumes of essays on Buddhism and craft, including *Turning the Wheel* (2007), *Taming the Ox* (2014), and *The Way of the Writer* (2016).

In life, as in his writing, Johnson does not limit himself to a single mode of approach. Born in

Evanston, Illinois, in 1948, he was raised in the African Methodist Episcopal Church; his youthful experiments with meditation led to a lifetime engagement with Buddhism and other Eastern traditions, including the study of Sanskrit and martial arts. He earned a B.S. in journalism and an M.A. in philosophy from Southern Illinois University and received a doctorate in philosophy and phenomenology from the State University of New York at Stony Brook. In 1976, Johnson was offered a position as assistant professor at the University of Washington, in Seattle, where he remained until 2009, retiring as the S. Wilson and Grace M. Pollock Professor. He has also had successful careers as a journalist and an illustrator.

In July 2016, Johnson and I spent two long afternoons together in the offices of the English department at the University of Washington. Our first conversation took place the day after an African American man opened fire on a group of police officers in Dallas, killing five and wounding nine. Johnson views race, like the distinction between forms, as an illusion, but with far greater consequences. "That young man was living out a narrative," he said. "He was living out a story, an interpretation of blacks and whites in America, today and in the past, going back to slavery. And he got caught up in an illusion filled with hate." Johnson was thorough, if professorial, in his consideration of craft, but it was in our discussion of the dharma, and meditation in particular, that he grew most animated. He was always eager to return the conversation to examples of lived experience, especially where it involved the joys and complexities of family life or the clash of cultures. "We can talk abstractly, we can talk sociologically and philosophically," he told me, "but this is ground zero. This is the way we're living."

—*Cary Goldstein*

INTERVIEWER

Of all your creative endeavors, which would you consider your first love?

JOHNSON

Well, art—drawing—preceded everything. From when I was a kid in the fifties, that was my passion, still is to a certain extent. By age fourteen or so, I told my dad I had figured out what I wanted to do with my life. I wanted to be an artist, a cartoonist and illustrator.

How did that go over?

My dad didn't know any artists, so he was very concerned about my future. He said, Chuck, they don't let black people do that. And that was pretty devastating for me because if I couldn't draw, I didn't want to live. But I saw an ad in *Writer's Digest* for cartooning classes with Lawrence Lariar and I wrote him a letter, just out of the clear blue. My dad says they don't let black people do this. Do you agree with that? I didn't expect to hear back, but a week later I got a fiery letter in which Lariar said, Your father's wrong, and you can do whatever you want, you just need a good teacher. I wrote back to Lariar and asked him to be my teacher. But of course, he didn't believe in free lunches, so he said, You have to pay for my course. It was a two-year course, what today we'd probably call distance learning, and my dad paid for it.

Were you always a reader?

My family has always valued education and skill acquisition, so I was a pretty avid reader from the time I was a kid. My mother had shelves and shelves of books. That's where I discovered Richard Wright. When I was going through the public schools, they were integrated but the curriculum was not. So teachers—white teachers—had never put before me a book by a black author. When I found *Black Boy* in my mother's collection, I thought, Am I supposed to read this? My teachers never mentioned it. Is it contraband? What is it? All of that was marginalized or erased from the public-school curriculum.

I remember she also had a book on yoga with a chapter on meditation. I was a pretty smart kid, so I sat down for half an hour and practiced what I'd read, and it was a remarkable experience, the most incredible thirty minutes I've ever spent in my life. I began studying everything I could about the Buddhadharma, all the way through my undergraduate years. And I was in a book club—a science-fiction book club—in high school. I loved science fiction. As a visual artist, literature stimulated my imagination. Cartoonists get tropes and metaphors from literature. So I was always reading.

What provoked your interest in philosophy?

I majored in journalism as an undergraduate at Southern Illinois University and took two philosophy courses. One was required—that was logic. The other was an elective about the pre-Socratics. It was remarkable. I'm listening to the professor and thinking, These are *my* questions. I have to stay close to these questions for the rest of my life. That class was seductive. In the journalism school, they told me I needed to stop taking those classes over there and finish up over here. So I did that. And when I graduated, I gave the degree to my dad and said, This journalism degree is for you. It proves I can make a living. Now I'm going to graduate school for philosophy, because that's for me. I worked as a journalist to support myself and my wife while I was working on my philosophy master's degree.

How did your studies in philosophy dovetail with your interest in Buddhism?

Well, let's start with the fact that fuzzy-bunny Buddhism doesn't often talk about what it's all really about—that it's a preparation for death. Buddhism begins with that young prince leading his sheltered life and seeing the four signs. He sees an old man, he sees a sick man, he sees a dead man, and he sees a holy man. And he realizes unequivocally, categorically, That's *me. I'm* going to get old, *I'm* going to get sick, and *I'm* going to die. So how do I deal with this? Buddhism is about letting go of a lot of conceptual baggage, the stories we tell ourselves about ourselves—you let that go and there's a sense of liberation and clarity.

Take Marcus Aurelius—*Meditations* got me through Stony Brook University. I'm a Ph.D. candidate, with the pressures of teaching undergraduates, passing my own graduate classes, my qualifying exam, and living in 1975 on my four-thousand-dollar assistantship, with a first child on the way, no job yet, and a second philosophical novel to complete that had to be more expansive than the first one. *Meditations* got me through because Marcus Aurelius understood suffering, impermanence, and death almost as well as a Zen master. And Plato once said that philosophy is really preparation for death. I extend that wisdom to our very notion of the self as an enduring entity. You let go of the things that are simply unnecessary, almost as Occam would, if indeed Occam used this phrase, "*Entia non sunt multiplicanda praeter necessitatem*"—"Entities should not be multiplied beyond necessity." David Hume figured this out—the self is not necessary. And Sartre figured it out—it is not necessary to posit an enduring, substantive self when we talk about human experience, and also it's empirically unverifiable. This is an important observation long recognized by Buddhists. This is what I care about. The word *philosophy* does mean, after all, the love of wisdom.

INTERVIEWER

When did you begin writing fiction?

JOHNSON

One of the challenges in my life has always been, I love this, I love that—how do I bring all the things I love together? I've had to reinvent myself about three times. First, as a cartoonist and visual artist in the sixties and early seventies. Then I hosted a TV show on PBS about drawing, *Charlie's Pad*, in 1970. And around that time, an idea came to me for a novel based on a kung-fu school that I went to in Chicago. I've been training in the martial arts since I was nineteen. But that first novel didn't turn out well—I wrote it very quickly over a summer.

INTERVIEWER

When you say that, you're not being humble?

JOHNSON

No, it wasn't very good. See, I would write a novel every ten weeks. I was trained in journalism—I was a stringer for the *Chicago Tribune* in 1969 and interned there during the summer of 1968. A newspaper journalist on staff has to file four or five stories a week. So I could do ten pages a day, sure, and I did that for two years, beginning with that first novel, two more, and then a trilogy, which is the last thing I worked on before I met John Gardner.

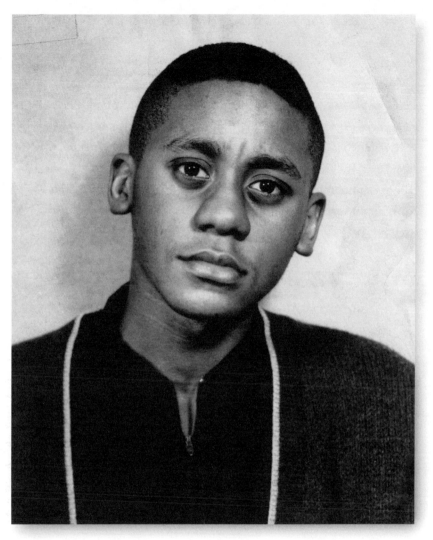

Johnson, in 1965.

How did you meet Gardner?

JOHNSON

I created comic strips with an English-major friend named Charles Gilpin—
he would write the scripts and I would draw them. I liked his irreverent sense
of humor. He had taken courses with Gardner and had started writing novels
himself. Chuck, me, and another guy would sometimes collaborate on comic
strips. *The God Squad* was one of them.

INTERVIEWER

Tell me about *The God Squad*.

JOHNSON

It was religious and social satire. We had an Adam and an Eve, but Adam was black. We had a monstrous creature in the Garden of Eden, the first fuckup God made before Adam—he had feet coming out of his shoulders. We had other characters who were amoeba-looking things that were souls in hell, and the devil was a cigar-smoking snake.

It was Gilpin who recommended that I read Gardner. By that time I was working on a master's in philosophy, and working at a paper called the *Southern Illinoisan*, where I did everything—features, a column, editorial cartoons, obits, interviews, farm news, and proofread the Sunday edition for eight hours on Saturday night. And that work was part-time, for fifty bucks a week, in 1971. So I'm sitting there at the paper reading the day's edition, and I see this ad for Gardner's course in professional writing. I called him up and asked if I could get into his class. He said, Sure, come on over. So I went over to his farmhouse, and it was a beginning class where everybody's sitting around a big coffee urn. Afterward, I put the six manuscripts I'd written on his table and he said, Well, what do you want with me? You can write. And I said, Well, yeah, but I think I could be better with things like voice and rhythm. And his response was, Oh, I can help you with that.

INTERVIEWER

Were you a fan of Gardner's?

JOHNSON

I had read *Grendel*. But a lot of the writers I liked when I was younger—John A. Williams, Richard Wright, Baldwin—were all realistic writers. And so I kind of fell into working very realistically for the first chapter of something I was fooling with, about a woman and her relationships with several men. I was bored by it and I gave it to John. I'm sitting there in his office and he's bored reading it and I was bored writing it and when I came home that night, I said to my wife—I think we were married two years by that time—I said, I need to get a rise out of this guy, and I know he's interested in philosophy. So I stayed up all night long writing twenty pages. I wanted to write not just a philosophical novel but a novel that was a celebration of storytelling itself, so it's in the form of a folktale. Before I went to bed, I went over to his office, slipped it under his door, drove back home, and went to sleep. Two o'clock in the afternoon I get a call—it's Gardner. He really likes these new pages. He said, You've got two chapters here instead of one. In other words, I needed to break it in half. And he was right. I wrote the first two chapters of the book as one chapter. So I did a rewrite, and that became *Faith and the Good Thing* (1974), my third book but my first novel, because it was preceded by two collections of political and racial humor, *Black Humor* in 1970 and *Half-Past Nation Time* in 1972. I wrote it over nine months, and he got me my agents, who I've been with since then.

INTERVIEWER

What did he teach you that helped you find your way into that story?

JOHNSON

I didn't know how to revise. I would write all the way through, and then I would write all the way through again, and then all the way through a third time, ten weeks at a time. He said, You've got to stay with this paragraph and make it right before you go on. For John, it's like you've got a glass and as you're revising and revising you're filling up the glass, and at some point it's going to spill over, by which I mean that through revision you make dis- coveries, you find puns and oracles in the language as you cut and layer each sentence over and over again. And you might, as you focus on the revision, even discover that you need to abandon your outline. So ninety percent of good writing is rewriting. I don't think first thought is always best thought— sometimes it is—but it's the hundredth thought that strikes me as the one you're looking for sometimes.

Working with John—and reading him—also helped me better under- stand what voice and rhythm were. That's how I got that sense of the musical- ity and the possibilities of the storyteller's voice in *Faith and the Good Thing*.

INTERVIEWER

From the first words of the novel we understand we're being told a tale—"Listen."

Like a grandparent talking to a child. It was fun to do, but I've never done that again. John wanted me to do another, bigger book like *Faith*, but, well, I'd gotten my rise out of John Gardner. The next book I had to do at that point was *Oxherding Tale* (1982). I had to go back and deal with all of the Eastern philosophy I had been consuming since the age of fourteen. It's not a book he understood because he was very Protestant, very Western. He thought Buddhism was wrong. That was a parting of the ways we had to make.

INTERVIEWER

Some of that Eastern stuff is in *Faith*, though.

JOHNSON

Some of it—classic Buddhist parables rewritten in the black American context. The character called the swamp woman is full of that kind of stuff.

INTERVIEWER

But nothing on the order of what you sought to achieve in *Oxherding Tale*.

JOHNSON

I published *Faith* with Viking, and my editor, Alan Williams, could not understand what I was doing with *Oxherding Tale*. I think it just freaked him out. When he first signed me up for *Faith*, he took me and my wife to a really nice restaurant. But then, when I'm working on *Oxherding Tale*, I come into New York City from Long Island and he takes me to a burger joint, right? A burger joint. That's how much our relationship was deteriorating. We go back to his office afterward and I listen to this guy's indifference to *Oxherding Tale*. I felt kind of devilish, so I said, Alan, you know what? I don't think I'm going to do this book after all, this *Oxherding Tale* book. I'd like to do a multigenerational black family drama. And his eyes lit up, he said, *That* I can take upstairs to the publisher. I went back out to Long Island, sat at my typewriter, and wrote Alan a letter, saying, I just floated that idea of a black cross-generational novel to see what you would say. The book I have to do is *Oxherding Tale*. Because if I couldn't do that, I would have no interest in writing fiction at all.

    That novel I often call my "platform" novel, referring to the Platform Sutra of the Sixth Patriarch of Buddhism, because it is the foundation of

all the work I've published since 1982. Alex Haley's *Roots* appeared around this time, so publishers wanted something on slavery, or multigenerational black this or that. PBS really milked that in the seventies, and I did work on many of these projects, like *Booker*, which received a Writers Guild Award for the best script in the category of children's television in 1985, and before that an episode of *Visions* called "Charlie Smith and the Fritter Tree," about the oldest living American. Now, *Oxherding Tale* is a slave narrative, yes. It has very specific conventions from the slave narrative as a literary genre. But it's really a philosophical slave narrative anchored in the most sophisticated Eastern thought, as well as Western.

INTERVIEWER

Late in the novel, you take a kind of authorial pause to talk about something called the "first-person universal." What is that?

JOHNSON

Oxherding Tale has two essay-ish chapters. The first one is on the nature of the slave narrative as a literary form, its conventions. The other one is called "The Manumission of First-Person Viewpoint," and in it I'm looking at the first-person narrator of the slave narrative and trying to ask questions about the "I." And it takes a kind of Buddhist turn. What is this "I"? Either the self is nothing or it's everything. That's where I introduce the term "first-person universal." In other words, it's meant to take us away from a Cartesian view of subjectivity.

INTERVIEWER

Oxherding Tale strikes me as the most complex of your novels, philosophically and structurally.

JOHNSON

It is more complex by twenty percent than *Middle Passage*, which followed it. I deliberately made my third novel less complex than *Ox*, wanting it to simply be an exuberant, though still philosophical, entertainment—first and foremost, a rousing sea adventure story. From the very beginning, when I was

A publicity photo for Johnson's 1970 PBS drawing series, *Charlie's Pad*.

studying philosophy, I wanted to write about ideas in a way that was reader friendly and didn't sound like something out of a philosophy seminar. So that was one of the things I was trying to do. And *Ox* took five years and twenty-four hundred pages. Then the next book, *Middle Passage*, six years, about three thousand pages. And then *Dreamer*, another seven years and three thousand pages. Because after *Faith and the Good Thing*, I realized what was at stake with every book. I want to produce my best thought, my best feeling, my best technique. I can produce copy—that's not a problem. I can produce books left and right. The question is, What do you want your name on? What do you want to endure?

INTERVIEWER

At what point do you have the inkling that you might have stumbled on a voice or a character or a story you're going to commit to?

JOHNSON

Because I know I'll have to live with it for a while—five years, six years, seven years—a novel has to have, at its core, a question so central that I'm going to keep returning to it because it's very important as a question *to me*. Every one of my four novels has a central question at the core. For *Faith and the Good Thing* it's, What is the good? I'm playing around with Plato's ideas about forms. What is the Form of the Good? And black people have a phrase, "the good thing." I give that to Faith, and she spins out this Candide-like journey looking for the good thing and gets all these men to respond to her with their interpretation of "the good thing." In *Oxherding Tale*, I'm looking for a better understanding of the self. What is it? In *Middle Passage*—where is home? For Rutherford that is a primary question. For the Africans in the novel, the Allmuseri, that isn't any concern, because they just left their home. But where is *his* home? And in *Dreamer*, the question is, How do we end social evil without creating new evil by our effort to end the old evil? Those questions are philosophically perennial. I'm not looking for a final answer. I want to explore the questions through the concreteness of character and plot and all of that. So I have to have a question that is central to my existential moment in time.

INTERVIEWER

What questions are on your mind now?

When I do the next novel, the question is going to be, What does it mean to be civilized? Or, What is civility? That's the question I care most about. I've been writing about it in essays and short stories, coming at it from different angles. I think increasingly in our moment right now, it's an open question. You've got the Islamic State, which has reinstated slavery for young girls, you've got the breakdown of civility among Americans—that's one thing people have been talking about for fifteen years.

INTERVIEWER

Look at the presidential-debate stages alone.

JOHNSON

Absolutely. The insults, the utter lack of civility from the Trump people. We've lost something. And so my question is, What does it mean to be civil? What kind of person do you have to be? That's an idea we can trace back through two thousand years of Western history, and the East as well, going back four or five thousand years. It's not a question that is going to go away. But in order to write a novel, you need a story, you need a plot. You must have the story first and foremost and then all of those ideas can come to the surface.

INTERVIEWER

Because *Faith* is a folktale, you get away with telling us on page one what the question is. Whereas in each of the books that follow, the characters are figuring out what the question is as the novels move along. And so the novels are, in a way, one large articulation of the question.

JOHNSON

I think you're right. A novel is a special site where philosophy and fiction can meet, and that's what I'm interested in. I'm not interested in writing novels for the sake of writing novels. I'm not interested in writing novels for the sake of having a career—I really have a problem with careerism. I was a college professor for thirty-three years, half my life, so I didn't have to write novels for money. I could do the kind of novels I wanted to do, that I felt would maybe fill a void in the American philosophical novel in general, but also in black American literature. The perennial, universal questions we have in the Western world and the Eastern world—How shall I live? What is the good life?—are about our most basic experiences as human beings. My job has been simply to expand upon, deepen, and explore those.

Which writers had the most direct influence on your work?

Writers who were philosophical in one way or another. Like Jean Toomer, especially in his book of aphorisms, *Essentials*, and in the poem "The Blue Meridian." He had an interest in Eastern thought. Richard Wright, of course, has a very strong philosophical orientation—well, he was Marxist, that's one thing, but also he was something of an existentialist. "The Man Who Lived Underground" is relentlessly existential. This comes before Ellison's *Invisible Man*, mind you. Whereas with Ellison you have a kind of exuberant—oh my God, very exuberant—Freudian tragicomic vision.

In writing philosophical fiction, is there a risk of having your characters seem like mere mouthpieces for ideas?

You can't be didactic. Ideas, for me, don't exist way up there in some Platonic realm. They're not abstract entities. Rather, because my background is phenomenology and, to some extent, existential phenomenology, I think ideas begin in the muck and mud of lived, daily experience. And for the purpose of reflection, we extract them so we can analyze them and talk about them. So when I write, I want return the ideas to their original source within our experience. You can find something philosophically interesting in the experience of slavery or the era of segregation. But even in our daily experiences, we walk around, go to the supermarket—that's where the ideas are grounded. And so my whole purpose is to bring it back to that and do what the novelist would do with it so we can see the ideas dramatized, tabernacled in flesh, and experience them on a level that's emotional as well as intellectual.

Once you've articulated your question, how do you begin making it into a novel?

JOHNSON

When the question is burning consistently within me, and over such a period of time that it won't leave me alone, I go to sleep and see characters, see scenes. I'm walking around and I'll see something and it'll immediately take me back to something I could do in the story I'm thinking about. So in other words, I have to feel it first, and then once I have what John Barth called the "ground situation"—the premise, the "conflict" is what people usually say—I've got something to work with. For a novel, it has to be a rich enough ground situation that it'll take me two hundred, three hundred pages, maybe five, six years to unpack it with all of the implications and possibilities or *energeia*—the potential that's inherent, as Aristotle would say—in the story. It's something I can meditate on, something I can keep coming back to, rewriting, discovering—discovering deeper and deeper layers of meaning in it. That's when I know I have a novel that is interesting to me.

INTERVIEWER

Do you outline?

JOHNSON

In the beginning I make a rough outline. Take my early outline for *Middle Passage*—you wouldn't even recognize the story line. I wrote a first draft in two years—a little fast. And then I had to go back for another four years and rethink it from the middle of the book to the end.

INTERVIEWER

Do you keep notebooks?

JOHNSON

Oh yeah. Notebooks and journals. The notebooks are my memory aides—I put something in them every day. I think I had three notations when I was working two nights ago. Phrases just came to me and I wrote them down and then pasted in an article with some information that I saw in the newspaper because it had some stats on educational levels for Asians and whites and blacks and Hispanics. I need to keep that as a reference. But this is not the same thing as a journal. With a journal you're actually writing your thoughts and feelings and you're dating that. I do some of that, too—a half page, a hundred words to myself on some subject that I think I've had some insight into. But the notebooks are scraps and fragments of information, descriptive stuff.

INTERVIEWER

How do you use them for your work?

JOHNSON

Once I have a draft started—five pages, ten pages—I go through them. I start with the first notebook.

INTERVIEWER

First notebook dating back to . . . ?

JOHNSON

They're all mixed up, but dating back to 1972. It's like thirty inches of material. Some of the stuff I haven't looked at in a long time. I'll start going through them and see a phrase, an image useful for the in-progress work. And it goes right into the manuscript.

INTERVIEWER

Do you cross things off to let yourself know you've used it?

JOHNSON

No, I don't cross it off. I look at the journals I kept in '72 and '73, when I was younger, and sometimes I'm surprised to see what was interesting to me so long ago. What kind of imagery or descriptions were interesting to me at age twenty-five? What emotional things were interesting to me at age thirty-five? But also I sometimes wonder, Why was I interested in that? Or, Why did *that* mean so much to me? It's like examining the spirit or soul of your younger self. But I might see one thought on a page in a workbook from 1990 and think, You know, that would work here in this new story. Or it might be a character description. A little concise thing that nails a character quickly for a reader in terms of physical description or a psychological description. And every day I'm putting something in there because I have thoughts and feelings and don't want to lose them. I will lose them if I don't write them down.

What was your approach to the workshop? And does it mirror your approach to your own work?

A self-portrait, made in 1992. "The perennial, universal questions we have in the Western world and the Eastern world—How shall I live? What is the good life?—my job has been simply to expand upon, deepen, and explore those."

JOHNSON

Well, I never took a creative-writing class, but I taught myself a lot about writing. In the early seventies, I read every book on the craft of writing I could get my hands on. And John sent me pages with exercises that wound up at the end of his posthumously published book *The Art of Fiction*. I had an idea of what a workshop should be, based on negative impressions I had of workshops I'd heard about. So when I got this job in Seattle, I made my students work, and they came out with around 140 pages by the end of a ten-week quarter. I taught with something akin to Gardneresque intensity. I threw myself into it because as I was teaching, I was learning. And that was helpful to me as I was working through *Oxherding Tale* and the short fiction. At Stony Brook I started the first story in *The Sorcerer's Apprentice* (1986), "The Education of Mingo," and I hit a wall. I couldn't finish it. I got a couple of paragraphs in, but I was cranking out seminar papers and my prospectus for my dissertation.

INTERVIEWER

You couldn't finish because you didn't know where it was going, or you didn't have time?

JOHNSON

I didn't have time, but in philosophy papers, you don't use metaphor and figurative language, so I was used to pulling back from that. When I got to Seattle, I taught my first short-story workshops, and by the second quarter, I was ready to write that story.

INTERVIEWER

You've written that the novel welcomes all forms—the low, the high, the transcendental, and the trashy. Are there any forms you want to experiment with that you haven't?

JOHNSON

You can have poetry in a novel. You can have many stories in a novel. You can tell tales. The novel is capacious because it doesn't have a rigid form. It's like Ishmael Reed once said, A novel can be the six o'clock news. There are rigid forms in genre fiction that you don't depart from, where you can't do everything. Like romance novels—they have very strict rules. But in a literary novel that's inventive, you can have stories within stories, like in *Faith and the Good Thing*, or forms within forms, as in *Dreamer* or *Oxherding Tale*. What was interesting to me about *Dreamer* was I could move from the third-person limited over King's shoulder—short chapters—to a first-person narrative. Once I understand the form I'm using, I can understand, in many ways, the content, where I need to go next. My notebooks are full of notations for myself on different forms that I might want to do. The one that keeps coming up for me, though, is the league novel, or *Bundesroman*—it's been in the back of my mind for twenty years.

INTERVIEWER

What is a league novel?

JOHNSON

The league novel was a popular pulp form in eighteenth-century Germany that generally involves a secret order of some kind. And as Gardner once said—I think he was right to a certain extent—a good deal of great American art is elevated trash. Hermann Hesse elevated the league novel in his book *Journey to the East*.

INTERVIEWER

Is Hesse an important writer for you?

JOHNSON

When I was younger I was drawn to Hesse, who was popular on college campuses in the sixties. I read his short stories and novels, and literary scholarship on his work, like that by Theodore Ziolkowski, who examined themes and structure in Hesse's fiction. I wanted to learn his method of composition, the way he thought. Hesse is interesting to me precisely because he works with different forms in his novels. He also has a spiritual dimension—he has us looking toward the East. A friend of mine gave me *Demian* when we were undergraduates. I wasn't really impressed. But it led me to *Siddhartha*. And then I thought, Here's a German in the 1920s writing about the Buddha and getting a good deal of it right. Man, that book so affected me. I really wanted to respond to it. And that response is, of course, *Oxherding Tale*. But what I did was respond from a black American perspective.

I used to give my grad students an assignment—I want a plot outline using a form that hasn't been used by a major work in a hundred years. Go to the library and research it. The way I see it, forms are our inheritance, our global inheritance.

And each form has its own conventions.

Well, if you want to know what I really think at this point in time—it may be strange to say this—I think that black literature has reached a point where it is full of exhausted conventions. The slave narrative and slave stories, for example. You're always going to have the master, evil or benign. You're going to have the slave who is content, you're going to have the slave who *isn't* content. There are conventions and threadbare tropes that come up again and again and again. And I wonder if that's a good thing. We have a tendency to exclusively interpret the black experience in terms of victimization—victimization and oppression. And if that's not in a story about black characters somewhere, or in a story about the black American experience, some readers will be disappointed, and ask, Where's the oppression? Where's the discrimination? It's an expectation that's drilled into us in terms of narratives about black Americans. I think it's racial and political kitsch.

My tendency is to acknowledge oppression but to also call forth other profiles of the black experience, because I know that black life, like all life, outstrips our perceptions, that so much of black life still remains—to invoke Ellison here—invisible, unseen. In my fiction, I have stories where you don't know what the character's race is. Or it's about a character who's black, but he's Martin Luther King Jr. and still a grad student finishing up his dissertation, like in "Dr. King's Refrigerator" (2005). He's got a new wife, and that's what the issue in the story is. He's spending too much time on his work, away from his wife, and so on. You get to the end of the story, after he's had a Buddhist epiphany about the interconnectedness of all things based on the food in his fridge, and you know within twelve months Rosa Parks is not going to give up her seat on a bus and he's going to become a "world-historical" figure, partly prepared for that role by his revelation a year earlier. Those are the human moments important to me—he's figuring out how to be married and how to deal with all the duties heaped upon a young minister. There doesn't have to be a big conflict, and there doesn't have to be a big *racial* conflict. I don't believe that's the totality of our experience.

INTERVIEWER

To put it another way, should a black writer have to write only for a black reader? Bellow wasn't writing for Jews, but he was writing about Jewish people.

JOHNSON

Exactly. Ellison and Bellow—they were friends, and Bellow was an early champion of Ellison. There's a similarity between those two guys that I think is very interesting. They both formulated some response to the question, What is the American novel? And here's Bellow, as a Jewish person, asking how the particulars of his experience could open up to a universal understanding. I mean, Jews were asking the same questions in the early twentieth century that black people were in the sixties. Should we assimilate or should we focus instead on our own culture and history? Well, Ellison was about the same thing—How do I talk about the American experience and the black experience so that you understand the American experience through the lens of black people? In other words, how do I achieve, in the particular, the universal in a philosophically interesting way? That's the issue for both of them. That's what makes them both great American novelists.

INTERVIEWER

How has the mission of American literature changed in the twenty-first century?

JOHNSON

American literature was a project. When the republic was formed, writers like Emerson were asking themselves questions about what it meant to be an American. We're a new land, we're a new people, we need a new literature. That conversation continued through the nineteenth century and into the twentieth with the infusion of more immigrants. I keep wanting to use the terms *aufgehoben* or *aufheben*, which Hegel uses to explain dialectical thinking, where you take something to a different level. Basically you start with two truths, antinomies—the truths of Jewish life or black life verses the WASP experience—and you find a synthesis that leads to a deeper understanding of America. But in the last thirty or forty years, our literature, in my opinion, has become balkanized. I believe some black authors write only for other black people. I remember one saying, If you want to listen in, white people, listen in, that's okay. Or it's a woman writing for other women. Or maybe it's Hispanics writing only for Hispanics. We have lost that sense of the *American* novel. As a practicing, lay Buddhist, an *upasaka* who took vows in the Soto Zen tradition, I do not have any interest in contributing to today's polarization, division, or divisiveness.

INTERVIEWER

Are there proprietary subjects in American literature? Are there topics or perspectives that are off-limits for exploration by someone who hasn't had that experience himself?

JOHNSON

It's tricky. The question is, Can you write outside of the cage of your race, class, gender, or cultural position? We're talking about it in terms of writing, but these are larger questions about America right now, and they're reflected in what we say about literature. Who has the right to write about, say, a black woman's experience? It's very complicated, and I don't quite know what to say. And as I said, I will write stories in which the race of the character is not important, a reader will not get any designations of that character's race, because race isn't important for the story. Or put it this way—we must, as writers, be able to empathize with the racial, class, gender, and cultural other. We must use our best research and imagination, as I try to do in a few stories in my new collection *Night Hawks*, to write stories about Muslim American soldiers, Japanese Zen abbots, black people, Plato and the Buddha, and stories that have no racial signatures at all.

INTERVIEWER

And yet, if you weren't black, you wouldn't have written the novels and stories you did.

In his office, with his grandson Emery, 2016. "I can produce copy—that's not a problem. I can produce books left and right. The question is, What do you want your name on? What do you want to endure?"

JOHNSON

No, I wouldn't be writing novels about the things I'm writing about. I am not blind to the illusion of race, I am not blind to American history and the history of race. But I'm not *bound* by these matters either.

Now, could I write about a white character? Yes, I could, and I have. Remember, I'm trained as a philosopher and a journalist—I had to learn how to take on any assignment. The reason you can't do this sometimes is because you don't know people. I've read that, overwhelmingly, white Americans live in neighborhoods or communities that are all white, so they don't have much personal contact with black Americans. They don't know us. They don't know how we talk. They don't know where we came from. They don't know our individual histories. They don't know our hearts. They have to project ideas on us that may have nothing to do with us whatsoever. This is the agony we're facing in America right now, so it's got to show up in our literature.

Why do you write?

I had never seen a book like *Oxherding Tale*. I'd never seen a book like *Middle Passage*. I'd never seen a book like *Dreamer*. I'd never seen stories like some of the stories that I've written, so I wrote them. I think a young writer should ask the question I ask myself—What can I bring to the table that nobody else is bringing to the table? Why am I doing this? *I'm* doing this because I believe I have a contribution to make to our philosophical literature. And when I say a philosophical literature, I mean a spiritual literature as well.

How do you know when you're done with a book?

You have to let it go, because if you didn't, you'd keep working on it, endlessly. I try to put everything I've got into a book for five, six years—it's got to be something I'm thinking about every bloody day, and it branches out to bring in other things, and when I'm done with it, I'm truly done with it. I don't go back and reread it. I don't look at it again, and there's not going to be a sequel. I guess the answer to when you know it's done is when you can't do anymore. You've gone over it until you have no more thoughts.

Do you ever imagine a time in which you'll no longer write?

I can't imagine it. There's no more thrilling process than creating. And that's all I ever wanted to do as a kid.

King, in *Dreamer*, feels that he's failed. He has a wish to live a simpler life. Is that something you have felt in some way?

I can easily relate to the need for a simpler, less cluttered life. That's how *Dreamer* opens—with King dreaming about going to Kerala, India. By the time *Dreamer* came out in 1998, I had been making a promise to myself for about ten, fifteen years that by the age of fifty all my duties, obligations, and responsibilities to everybody in my life from childhood forward would finally be discharged. Every bloody one. Period. I worked to serve others— family, colleagues, friends, students, the book world—as completely as possible. To stay "at my post," as Emerson put it. Then, at age fifty, I promised myself that I would be free to step back or away from these social obligations and allow my commitments to the Buddhadharma to deepen. I'm only just realizing that goal, but now I want to spend my time, this winter season of my life, in spiritual practice, creating, learning—I am a lifelong learner—and just writing about the things I love.

Nick Laird

AUTOCOMPLETE

I expect the holy of holies must be
to watch machinery making machinery,

no? Begin with the others and do what they do,
and later you can branch off into the fresh

snow. Did you think the room smelt of not
having been smoked in? Or that she had a face

like the gate of a pool after closing? The wax seal
began as a personal stamp of authenticity before

it grew into a tool the administrators used
to represent you. Given the soul's freehold meant

setting up franchises across the different sites. I
would like to swim in you, it's true, and I would add

that you should feel free to look me in the eyes when I do
so.

The Wait

JOANNA NOVAK

The moist cheese on his blue-and-white porcelain, the Pinot.

Our entire marriage, I had been accepting those gifts, not waiting for the meal. My husband came into the living room and sniffed behind my ear. He moved my pretty hair. He told me I smelled like a newborn. Not baby powder: it was something else about me.

Did you ever find pineapples? he asked. For Sunday?

No.

You better go back. Otherwise it's on the list with the playing cards.

What?

I'm kidding, he said.

He handed me that sweaty cheese.

I want to wait for dinner, I said. He left the wine on the arm of the sofa. I sat there, watching the kitchen fill with steam.

And that's how I coddled the wait. It was a misfit infant coming, no matter how slowly or quickly I ate my supper.

Both this phantom infant and I wanted to separate from my husband.

You'll get your wish, I told the infant.

I poured the wine my husband gave me out the window, where it ran red on the asphalt.

A turgid thunk came from the kitchen: that was my husband, slow at the cutting board.

Meanwhile, the wait was developing a smell, of starch coming off pasta. And it had its sound, the hidden purr of boiling water. Our timer was a cat, one of those Japanese good-luck charms with crazy eyes.

It rang and the pasta was poured into a colander.

I did not need to be in the kitchen with my husband to know that he was waiting for the water to run off the noodles before he returned them to the pot. Shook them. Sauced them.

We were not waiting for the same thing, and maybe we never had been. Except, perhaps, once. There was the time he had told me to undress and crawl from the kitchen to the bedroom so he could watch my ass, to wait for him at the foot of the bed, on all fours. I did.

Then it was dinner. Absolutely, the wait was there, sitting at the table like an awful baby or a pepper mill. I could not tell if it was across from me, around me, riding my back like a coat.

Heat rose off the noodles and I fought back speech.

The food was still too warm to taste. I needed something for my mouth. The wine, I guess. The sheep's Brie I'd turned down. Perhaps I'd developed this tendency in the early days of love when we'd waited out halftime ads, his penis in my mouth.

By "tendency," I probably mean habit.

Ritual, like whacking your thumb every morning with a hammer and hiding the pain with your tongue.

Ten faces, ten colors, my husband said, looking at me looking at my food. It was a common saying in Japan, and he'd been using it since he was twenty, when he'd spent a year there doing voice work for a pocket-dictionary publisher. He held up his glass and went on: To us and our missing pineapple and our cat egg timer.

Damn he was good. He toasted every night, and here I was, waiting for a noodle to leap off the table. I dawdled with my fork.

Is it all right? he asked.

Just not hungry, I said.

I dabbed my mouth with my napkin and got it red.

All along, I hadn't been waiting but awaiting. I was awaiting discovery, awaiting someone who would sweep up all my crumbs and re-create a cake. I had ruined the napkin. I had tossed the wine.

What would I have to do?

I'm waiting, my husband said, drawing out the word, singsong.

Waiting, awaiting.

Now, when you bring me to your different bed, I slow myself from desiring you, new person. Ceremony, like patience, is a dark art. Two bodies needn't share a meal. I ask you to crawl for me, come for me, and I am so hopeful, with my flat, empty stomach. When it starts to talk, I tell myself to keep waiting. That's it. I wait for everything you do.

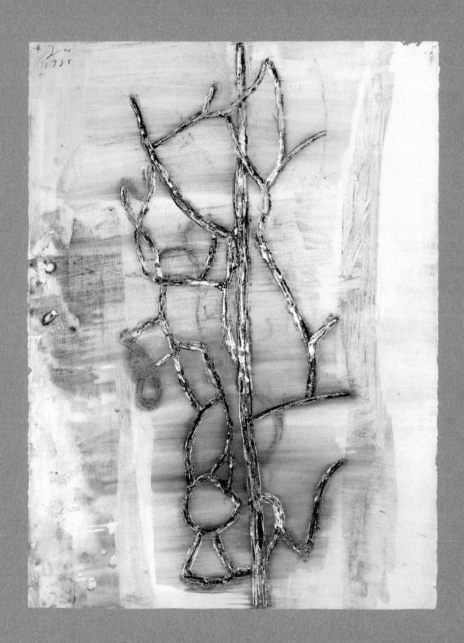

Untitled, 1988, gouache and charcoal on paper, 30" x 22".

Poems by Peter Cole, Drawings by Terry Winters

from "A WINTERS TRAIL"

Drawing draws us in-
volving us further and stretching
attention it sketches reaching
inching in ink and grasping
graphite graphing drawing
draws us out of our cells
and selves extending thinking
into seeing what was
sensed or seen as something
once in hand an eye
or at the fingers' tips
it leads one on to a place
of twos and too and into
depths and arcs as angles
curve through layered swerves
and lines as tines drawing
is first and quickest to
the quick and draw and yet it
slows and flows unfolding
time raveling mine it
tries out signs along
a way a wavering it's
a doodle dancing within
its perfect incompletion
now a mesh and not a
mess a net that's working
through a seam between us
drawing seems to hone
what might be true and turn

Untitled, 2009, graphite and gouache on paper, 22" x 30".

by turn it trains but doesn't
tame. Like runes. It tunes us.

*

There is a score to all
that isn't said a constant
buzz or hum enlarged
a pulse that soon becomes
like something sung or spoken
within there is a string
no, there are wavering
violins we bring
a tension like a wish
a wind along a wall
or laundry line and clothespins
marking time with keys
shifting through an un-
quaint calm and now
a chaos of tangled thinking's
twine, in a drawer,
a silent roar the world
is bound by secret knots,
they say, though what that means
is hard to know and flickers
so, also, and really
are those knots a noose
that hangs or ties that bind
our being stuck or held
together like a bridge
to build and cross or maybe
draw on or up
so no one can there is
a score to all that...

Animation, 1996, charcoal, graphite, and oil on paper, 41 ⅝" x 29 ¾".

*

This writing's on and off the wall
and tells us what it is and why
we're so   intent on understanding
a layered saying that seems to say it
all and nothing in particular
just like everything seen by those
who know it shows at best the whole
in part that's growing with the telling
and spell   dangling   in between
like someone listening into a
certain sort of uncertainty speaking
of uncertainty as a song
of songs truly tangled in our
being led along a luminous
line singed and limned within
the singing's seeing seeing us through

*

This world's dotty matrix calls
    and draws us toward a broken cause's
lozenged rose or window wall
    and whorl or just a kind of clausal
contract with the viewer you
    might be paying attention now
to the verb itself as somehow
    pay implies a currency in
a thicker economy of concentration
    and price that rhymes with sacrifice
which may be why these vortices bear
    spheres and diamonds in their whir
this morning's something we almost feel
    or feel but can't quite put into words

Untitled (Page), 2011, graphite on paper, 11″ x 8 ½″.

or give a name to   and that's the pearl
　　a cone of dark that lets light through
a future via repetition's
　　asking once and then again
a tension's moving around within
　　what might be only a fancy screen
savored and caught in a nick of Time
　　on a page we drift across
the day and toward its deckled edge
　　giving way to what it suggests—
beauty's keeping secrets between us
　　or screaming in silence to be seen
making a music of its emergency
　　sail to a small magnificence or
this eddy's swirl's a pendant to
　　a listening that's an end and means:
an eerie earring funneling care
　　as hours that are always theres.

OK, Mr. Field
Part 2 (Autumn)

—

KATHARINE KILALEA

ILLUSTRATED BY
KYLE HENDERSON

IN OUR PREVIOUS INSTALLMENT . . .

*Mr. Field, a concert pianist, splinters his wrist in
a train crash and uses his compensation to buy a
house he has seen only in photographs: a replica of
Le Corbusier's Villa Savoye on a stretch of coast
outside Cape Town. He moves there with his wife,
Mim, and within weeks, the house begins to have a
disturbing effect on him. Its glass walls and open-
plan spaces estrange the couple, while its unusually
narrow windows, which, like a peep show, hold their
contents tantalizingly out of view, excite him. As
time passes, his thoughts are drawn, repeatedly, to a
brief encounter with the house's previous inhabitant,
Hannah Kallenbach, with whom he felt an unusual
intimacy. Then, one night, without warning or expla-
nation, Mim leaves.*

V

The capacity to love

Autumn arrived with a general spray of autumn color. It wasn't winter yet, but it would be; there was a hint in the air of the cold to follow. The village was quiet. The cafés had covered their tables and upturned their chairs and the ice-cream shop had its roller shutters pulled shut. Waiters at the fish-and-chip shop loitered around with nobody to serve. The holidaymakers who'd swarmed the bead shops and art galleries (*I'm looking for a painting with ocher in it, something to go with my Indian silk curtains*) had covered their sofas, locked their houses, and left.

I hadn't liked the holidaymakers. I hadn't liked the way they clogged up the roads with their expensive cars and sat around in cafés—the men in cricket hats and the women with their hair curled under—staring at the sea over the tops of their newspapers with their mouths open as though they were so at ease with themselves that they'd forgotten they were in public. All summer I'd longed for them to be gone but when the cavalcade of motorbikes and white sedans towing boats made its way out along the road toward Cape Town, I regretted their leaving. Surrounded by deserted roads and deserted windows, I felt like I'd been separated from the total mass of the population, like someone left in an environment that wasn't intended for humans anymore.

I thought of Mim, but not often. I missed her, but in an ordinary way. I didn't pine for her. I didn't miss her in the way you're meant to miss someone you love. And the truth is that sometimes I even enjoyed the small, unforeseen pleasures of my situation. Like the quiet, or the predictability of days spent alone, or being able to walk around the house naked without it seeming sexual. But there were times in bed, when my feet couldn't find hers to warm themselves against, when all at once my body would register her absence with such shock that I'd go to the window and stare at the empty parking space where her car used to be as though its return were somehow more likely if my gaze was there, waiting for it.

Sometimes, in the afternoons, which were a lonely time, I'd go down to the café. Sitting among the families eating and couples fighting and friends

---

The Paris Review is publishing *OK, Mr. Field* in its entirety over the space of three issues. A hardcover edition will appear in July from Tim Duggan Books.

meeting for coffee, I'd find myself thinking, though not explicitly, about myself. Or rather, thinking about myself in relation to them. *They are so much better than me*, I'd be thinking. Because as I watched people eating and talking and letting their knees touch under the table, the banal phenomena that are repeated in almost exactly the same way by hundreds of people day in, day out, I was, all the time, making comparisons between myself and them. I watched how long it took people to eat compared to me and thought, *What's the matter with me, why am I so hungry?* I watched people adjusting their hair with their hands and thought, *How often do they touch their hair compared to me?* I watched friends exchanging platitudes and thought, *How bored they look, sitting there. Do they like being together? Why do they choose to spend time with each other rather than being alone?* I watched mothers feeding their children and answering their childish questions and thought, *What is it about having children that gives people pleasure?* Perhaps they liked teaching them things. Then I saw a boy touching his mother's face and playing with her hair and thought, *It must be nice to be adored in that way.*

One afternoon, encircled by strange thoughts like these, I left the house. Instead of taking the coastal road into the village, I made my way along the dirt path that led through the nature reserve on the mountain. The trail was easy and popular with tourists; in summer it was overrun with rosy-faced holidaymakers in hiking gear, but that afternoon, although the cold and the winds had not yet set in, the car park had only the odd car in it, and the path itself was empty apart from a few people shuffling around in raincoats.

The path had started out in the direction of the village but it soon became apparent that it didn't lead toward it, or if it did, it did so indirectly, circling toward its destination via a series of staircases and diversions. I walked slowly. All around me—the end of the day was looming—was white grass yellowing, green grass lightening to a yellower, more luminous green. Birds, invisible in some tree, were squawking. I was alert to people passing. I saw joggers and women walking in pairs, their shadows mingling with mine on the path. I saw rock rabbits. I saw a picture of a lost dog taped to a tree and this, for some reason, seemed significant. Leathery shrubs with pale-pink flowers poked from the rock face.

After meandering for an hour or so along the side of the mountain, the path dipped through a forest. It climbed for a while upward, over some rockier terrain, and then the trail branched. The arrow pointing downward read CABLE CAR, and the one pointing up read HARBOR. Above me the cable-car building stood out grandly against the emptiness of the sky. There were no birds or airplanes, just air thickening into dense gray clouds. The light was changing. I stopped, looking down on the bay. Perhaps the choice of route had gotten confused with some more significant decision in my mind because I stood there for some time looking upward and then downward and then upward again. Who knows how long I'd have gone on standing there had not a group of teenagers suddenly appeared. They were smoking and I felt afraid to be alone, with nobody to know that I was gone, no one waiting for me. One of the boys spoke to me in a language I didn't understand, though I could tell from his rising inflections that he wanted something. *No*, I said. He spoke again and again I said *no*. Then, because they chose the higher path, I took the lower.

The path started off down the slope but turned back on itself after a few minutes before narrowing and entering a ravine so encroached upon by overgrown bushes and trees that it felt less like a path than a tunnel. The sun was setting in earnest now. Something about the time of day and the time of year—like hinges between day and night and summer and autumn—seemed to unhinge me, too. I knew where I was but at the same time I had only a vague sense of where I was. Beneath me some amalgam of the failing light and humidity had dematerialized the sea, turning it and the sky into a single gray mass. The rocks, which earlier had been too bright to look at without squinting, grew formless. Shadows came alive with small animals diving away into other shadows. As the light gave way, objects slipped their boundaries, and as they did my thoughts blurred, as though seeing and thinking were connected, so that not being able to see clearly meant not being able to think clearly either. I began to make out, I thought, a shape on the path. It looked like somebody walking ahead of me but it was just a long black strip, so it was hard to tell whether they were coming closer from somewhere very distant or the opposite, if they were almost almost gone. My heart sped up because although it wasn't Mim—of course not—in the dark, when a person is reduced to the shape of their hair or the colors they usually wear, figures are just figures, and every upright figure could be the person you long for and have been hoping to see.

I walked quickly, following the walker, trusting him or her to lead me somewhere, and before long, hemmed in on either side by black shrubs and black rocks and black foliage, I lost my bearings on the narrow, turning path. Once, as a child, my parents had taken me to the Duomo in Milan. Having paid a few lira, we joined the crowds climbing the long spiral staircase to the roof of the cathedral, which offered panoramic views of the city. I remember the sign outside the cathedral as having read FROM THE HIGHEST LOVE COMES THE MOST SHATTERING BLISS, though I suppose it couldn't really have said that. The stairwell was dark and narrow and ascended in a gently sloping spiral; the only light was the light coming in from the slitted embrasures cut into the thick stone wall. I could see only the two or three steps directly ahead of me and the windows were so far above eye level that it was impossible to gauge, in relation to the outside world, how far I'd climbed. The cathedral had looked stumpy from outside but must have been quite tall because I seemed to be climbing endlessly and became so dizzy and claustrophobic from going round in circles that at one point I tried to turn around, but the stairwell was too narrow to squeeze back past the queue of people behind me, so I kept climbing, feeling with each turning step that I was becoming more submerged, more cut off from the world, as though the farther up I climbed the further inward I was going, as if with each stair I was moving deeper into my own body or the maze of my mind.

The mountain path was still lined on either side by a combination of trees and some kind of dense mountain hedge. From time to time I stopped and looked around but all I could see in the dim light were differentiated shades of black and, occasionally, through what must have been a gap in the leaves, the flecked edges of the sea. The path rose higher along the side of the mountain then leveled out, its contours dissolving into the ridge, which dropped off sharply beneath me. The air was blood temperature. A cloud of mosquitoes hovered around me and I, because all my attention was on where next to place my feet, let myself be eaten. I had the impression, as if in a dream, that somewhere nearby a dog was driving a few cattle up the mountain.

The stars had disappeared so completely behind the clouds that I didn't see the little cottage until it was right in front of me. It was a plain rectangular building, painted black or built from very dark brown timber, like a fisherman's cottage. Its lights, if it had any, were off, so that like everything else, it was swallowed into the general darkness. The cottage had two doors, a wooden inner door and a netted screen to stop insects, which bounced shut behind me. As the clouds shifted, a strip of dust was illuminated by a beam of moonlight cutting through the room. There were some furnishings inside but not enough to live by: a dining chair but no table, a television but no sofa.

Baboons must have ransacked the cupboards because bits of broken glass and half-eaten food were trodden into the floor. On the counter was an aubergine so misshapen it must have been months old. I thought of a story in the *False Bay Echo* about an old lady, *Mrs. So-and-So from Capri Road*, who'd been at home one night, tending to her fire, when two men broke in. They tied her hands with the toaster cord and removed her jewelry. *Don't make a fuss*, they told her, *or we'll cut off your head—swish—with a knife*. They took whatever they could, including her furniture. She relaxed her finger so they could take off her wedding ring. *They took it gently*, she said, *like it was made of glass. They took it so carefully that I felt no panic. In fact, I felt so calm, lying there on the carpet, that I was tempted to just stay there and go to sleep in front of the fire.*

I was relieved, shortly after leaving the cottage, to encounter an elderly German hiker who directed me back down the mountain. The path terminated not at the car park but on a stretch of pavement beside the sea. Ahead of me, across the bay, I saw the village. Sounds drifted across the water, the sounds of dishwashers and kitchen porters singing and clapping their hands as they cleaned away plates. How wonderful their singing sounded. It presented something to get closer to. It gave a shape to a journey that, until then, had seemed endless. As I walked I tried to sing—and why not, there was nobody to hear me—but my voice seemed to be far down in my chest and when I opened my mouth all that came out was a kind of barking sound, as though I was trying to cough up something that wouldn't come.

The tide was low. Gulls turned in slow arcs overhead. Fishermen came off their boats with their trousers rolled up. *Yellowtail! Yellowtail! Yellowtail! Yellowtail!* they said as they off-loaded their catch onto their tarpaulins. I watched a fisherman trap a fish beneath his foot and cut a half-moon under its mouth. *Rosie*, he said, throwing the innards into the sea, *come and get your dinner*. A seal who'd been floating in the water with her chest upturned flopped over and swam to the pier. She climbed out and came right up to him, taking the fish and slapping her fins together as if to say *thank you. Now, Rosie*, said the fisherman, *you must go and share with your family*. Which she did, letting the fish loose in the water for the cubs, who crowded round snatching bits of flesh.

A yellow-haired waiter standing outside the café smiled at me so genuinely as I passed, his whole face lighting up, that I couldn't help going in. People were talking and laughing. In the kitchen a chef tossed a skillet over an open flame. Barmen unpacked boxes of wine piled onto the black-and-white-checkered floor. I thought of Mim and put myself down on whatever chair was nearest. *Where was she?* I tried to picture her somewhere (because a person who actually exists must *be somewhere*) but since all I knew for certain was that she'd driven off, the only image I could conjure up was a picture of her sitting in the car. *I ought to telephone her*, I thought, *so she's not so lonely.* All the muscles in my legs were tense, as though suspecting the chair beneath me might be about to collapse.

The yellow-haired waiter put down a basket of rolls and some butter that had been out of the fridge for some time. *What can I do for you, my love?* he said, and it was just a turn of phrase of course, but I blushed because all at once I had the idea that I would like to be loved, or if not loved then at least liked by him. *No more mussels*, he said. *No more mussels, no more kidneys.* How can you tell if someone would like to be loved by you? Who knows. But maybe! He wore rough cotton trousers with a drawstring waist and a shirt woven from a thread so fine you could see right through to his chest. The menu was stuck to the remains of someone's spilled drink. *Are you hungry?* he asked, and I suppose I was because there was a pain in my stomach, which is where Mim's absence had located itself, in my empty stomach with no food to temper it.

Two overweight women eating at a nearby table looked up. They seemed to be looking at me but were in fact looking at the wall behind me, which served as a makeshift gallery for local artists. The painting which interested them was on the top right-hand corner of the wall, a faux-religious image of a modern-day Mary and Joseph kissing on a rugged outcrop of rocks in front of the sea. Mary and Joseph were kissing passionately, as though in the process of being separated or reunited (you could tell they were holy from the glow around their heads), but the fact that the rocks they were standing on looked like sirloin steaks undermined any sexual feeling. The overlap of their kissing faces, painted in a flat, almost cubist style, merged into the illusion of a third face that was wonky and dislocated.

Beneath the picture of Mary and Joseph were several portraits which I thought at first were of a number of women with a physical likeness—all large and bald—but in fact all depicted the same woman, just in different painterly styles and poses, sometimes clothed, sometimes naked, sometimes smoking a cigarette, et cetera. Something about the painter's attention—a mixture of cruelty and curiosity—was strangely titillating and I couldn't help wondering who the woman was and why the painter had painted her over and over again. The exquisitely intimate nature of his gaze invited one to fantasize a narrative for their situation: A man paints a woman. While he paints she looks at him looking at her. He paints her again and again, not because he finds her sexually attractive (she is, after all, a very large and totally hairless woman) but because he likes being looked at in that way. Seen like this, the act of painting was a kind of seduction, not an erotic seduction (though sometimes she seems to be looking seductively at him from the canvas) but a sort of visual intercourse, the painter's way of keeping them alone together in the room. There was something disturbing about the portraits. Traveling across the row of paintings, I kept hoping that something would change, that the intensity of the painter's gaze would lessen, that his desire to paint, like the paint itself, would eventually run out. But he seemed to want to go on painting her forever.

Across from me was a man with brown stains on his fingers who was sitting alone. *Excuse me*, he said to the waiter. His accent was thick and he spoke with some difficulty, as if he'd had a stroke. *Excuse me*, he said again. *Can my dog come in?* He pointed outside to a tied-up dog licking itself on the pavement. The dog looked up as if knowing it was being discussed. *It depends*, said the waiter. *Is it the kind of dog that just sits under the table? What kind of dog is that*, the man said, *a dog that's under sedation?* The dog was small and had a stump instead of a tail. It looked happy, happy but with no tail to wag. *I like dogs*, said the waiter, *but I prefer the ones with short hair. A dog is a reason to have conversations with people*, the man said, *about the dog, and beyond.* Then the dog came in and it didn't cause any trouble.

Outside, a family of seals was sleeping on the rocks. The waiter delivered a portion of squid to a group of people sitting nearby. *Mmm*, a man said, *it's so tender. How do you get it so tender?* The waiter said they tenderized it by beating it to death against the rocks. *Ouch!* the man said. *Do they cry? How do squids cry?* the waiter replied. Through the window, boats were sailing in and out of the bay, little boats sailing in behind the big trawlers, as if dragged in their wake. A swarm of seagulls followed the boats, trailing the scent of fish, their white underbellies flashing in the moonlight. The waiter arrived with my food and said, *It's beautiful, isn't it? I love rocks, they're so peaceful.* He put his hand on the back of my chair and poured me a glass of Pinotage. He was *a connoisseur of Pinotage*, he said. As I swirled the wine in my glass, he noticed my wrist, cocked at an unusual angle. *What happened?* he said. *Nothing*, I said. *Nothing serious. Is it painful?* he asked. *It looks painful. Perhaps a glass of wine will make you feel better.* I looked at the moon, the fast-moving clouds, the moonlight on the water. *Nobody cares about one's personal trials and griefs*, I thought. *One's trials and griefs are boring.*

But actually, at that very moment, the two women eating nearby—Flo and Dot—were having a miserable conversation that was deeply interesting. Flo was fleshy and had a necklace tan. Dot looked like a librarian and had a bun that wanted to come undone. It appeared that Flo had lent money to Dot, who didn't have the money to repay her. Dot's lips were drawn in a line over her teeth as if to stop whatever she had to say from spilling out. Flo was philosophical. *Don't worry about the money*, she said, *the money will come.* But Dot was saying, *I'm sorry, I'm sorry, I'm sorry, I'm sorry* and gripping the menu as though the pressure of her fingers was holding everything together. *What are you sorry about?* Flo said. *What do you have to feel sorry for? Everything will be okay in the end.* They'd been drinking all night, so when the music changed it didn't take much encouragement for Dot to stand up and start dancing, rocking from side to side, raising one leg and then the other in a sort of gumboot dance. At first I turned away, because dancing embarrasses me, but then, because Dot was such a beautiful dancer—the way her body moved was just so *joyful*—I didn't have it in me not to look. After a while Flo started dancing, too, but her limbs were awkward and disconnected, like an insect dancing on its hind legs, so that it looked less like a dance and more like a struggle. When the chorus came on—*Looking from the window above, it's like a story of love*—Dot opened her arms in the general direction of the restaurant in a gesture which seemed to say, *Come into me. All the folds of my soul are open to you*, then leaned over and seemed, although I'm sure I'm wrong about this, to be showing us her ass.

VI

You see, Touw thought he could divine water

At eight the next morning I woke to the sound of the chain securing the construction site rattling as it fell to the ground. Then a thudding began which stopped a second later only to resume a minute or so after that. I pulled the duvet over my head but the fabric seemed to amplify the sound rather than muffle it. In any case, the orchestration of banging was so unpredictable—it had no rhythm or sonic organization at all—that it was impossible to sleep because all I could think about was the thudding; even when it stopped I was just waiting for it to start up again.

I went up to the solarium. For weeks the construction site had been quiet. The surveyors had come and done their surveys and the only other activity was somebody occasionally shifting the digger from one side of the site to the other. But now, when I looked behind the house, as though somebody had come overnight and cut away the mountain with a razor, all that was there was a flat plane with a metal storage container on it. Two men in yellow vests were walking around the site. One made his way along the side closest to the fence with an armful of pegs (long metal sticks folded at one end), pushing their tips into the earth at regular intervals, while the other, following behind, knocked them in with a maul.

Through the smell of construction came the smell of the sea. The sea that morning was a uniform nothingness with a purple-gray hue. Dense gray clouds were rolling in. The voice in my head, Hannah Kallenbach's voice, said, *It wants to be a storm*. But for me the clouds held no more shape than a dream. What can a man say about a cloud without sounding like a fool? The dried-up herbs in the planter looked gray. When the sun withdrew behind the clouds, my old white T-shirt looked gray and the concrete slabs lying by the side of the road looked doubly gray. The man with the maul, who gazed up from time to time, his eyes sunk into their deep gray sockets, at the length of land still to be pegged, looked like a character from a Cold War film. Gray trees. Gray trees and houses. All around, as the clouds moved, one species of gray gave way to another. It dulled things, yet the overall effect was not dull. It was compelling somehow to sit there, just registering these shifts. The weight of the clouds didn't dilute the light. Quite the opposite, it distilled it. Since although the light—that of it which emerged through the thick canopy of clouds—had lost its brightness, it had, at the same time, acquired an intensity and restraint, as if in struggling through the clouds it had acquired something of their density.

The man with the maul had taken off his vest and the sea haze made the edges of his body waver as in a mirage. I watched him the way the holiday-makers watched the sea: pruriently, letting my face slacken. Perhaps the earth

had been compacted by the diggers because sometimes he had to bring the maul down on a peg several times before the soil gave up and let it in. There was, I thought, something humiliating about the business of hitting in pegs, something about the way the pegs just stood there, waiting to be hit in. Or how the man with the maul said, *Stand still so I can hit you* when he hit a peg at a bad angle and it shied away from him.

Above me the sun flickered through the clouds as though its filament was about to wear out. I left the solarium and entered the living room, causing my old Bechstein to rock and let out its confused, imploring sound. The piano, I had always thought, was the simpleton of the musical world, sounding off at the slightest provocation. Not like the oboe or clarinet, which strained just to produce a note. Nevertheless, I sat down and opened a score by some dull composer, Czerny probably, and started playing. The piano had developed an echo on the high notes which lingered in the air, and I hadn't played for so long that my fingers felt arthritic, moving along the keys in a stiff and lifeless way, an impression heightened by my wrist, which hovered so awkwardly over the keys that it seemed to me the broken bones must have been fused back together at an incorrect angle. It was cold. I stopped playing to adjust the radiator then sat down again. Several times I stood up to fetch a blanket or adjust the piano stool or straighten the leg of my pajama trousers (which always bunched beneath me), then sat down again only to find myself standing up a moment later to make some or other minor shift in my environment. This compulsive getting up and sitting down continued for some time until, unable to make myself comfortable, I closed the lid and went back to the solarium. The men in yellow vests were still snaking their way up and down the site with their pegs. They worked together. When a row of pegs had been knocked in, the man with the maul came along with a ball of green twine which he attached to the tops of the pegs to create a long green line. First they rationalized the site into a series of green lines. Then, beginning from a northerly direction, they created a series of perpendicular green lines which crossed the original lines at right angles. It became apparent, as the process of unraveling the twine advanced, that they were dividing the site into a grid. The coordinates, I imagined, for some as yet nonexistent underground activity—the gas lines, perhaps, or the sewage system.

Later in the afternoon, as the sun was dropping behind the mountain, I returned to the piano, angled the task light down, covered my legs with the blanket, and tried again. In the dusky light, the notes wavered on the stave. My playing was accompanied by the regular beat of the builders hitting in pegs, though from inside the house the sound was distant and detached, and more defeated somehow. When I stopped to listen to it, it seemed to me that what I heard was not a thud so much as a low ticking sound, as if the old wooden metronome that had accompanied my boyhood practice sessions had returned now to restrain me from getting carried away by whatever I was playing. The memory of those long and lonely afternoons spent holed up in a practice room with that implacable tick made my heart strain. *It isn't natural to be shut up like that with just a piano for company*, Hannah Kallenbach said. To pass the time I'd tape a sheet of paper over the door window and masturbate, so that to this day the act of masturbation and metronomes are indelibly connected in my mind. *It takes its toll on someone*, said Hannah Kallenbach, *to be alone like that for hours, months, years… It makes sense that a person who has spent so much time alone in a room, over time, would come to believe that a room could give him nothing but solitude.*

It took all afternoon for the grid to be fully realized and at the end of the day Touw arrived. He stood to one side, leaning against the fence with his arms crossed. The site looked like it had been covered by a mesh or a loose green weave. He drank a can of something and smashed his boot against a block of paving with an expression of deep concentration. After a few minutes of doing this he crouched down and exclaimed, *Here, I can feel it. I feel the pull of the paranormal. There's a river here*, he called to the workmen. *What should we do with it?* Suddenly I brushed up against a forgotten dream. There was a pause between recalling the existence of the dream and recovering its contents. The dream concerned Hannah Kallenbach, though it was not Hannah Kallenbach herself who formed the subject of the dream so much as the room at the back of her house. I'd dreamed I was walking toward the yellow room along a corridor, only the corridor, with a dreamlike disrespect for proportion, had grown so long (like the corridors in the Houses of Parliament, with countless doors opening off either side) that I knew I would never reach it. There seemed, in fact, to be a number of interconnected dreams about the yellow room, or rather its absence. In one dream I reached the door only to find the wood so swollen and the handle so stiff that it wouldn't open. In another I forced the door open only to find the room behind it completely unrecognizable, its walls clad in oppressive wood panels and lined with fax machines and TVs all tuned in to different channels, like some kind of broadcasting station.

Outside, someone shouted and a car door closed with a deep thud. The chain on the gate rattled as the builders locked up to go home. I sat down on the chaise. The temperature was dropping—it was colder than it had been at one or two o'clock—and the radiator just hummed and whined and issued a damp stream of air into the room. The coldness tired me. Although perhaps it wasn't the coldness that tired me so much as the house, since there is an idea that a house should afford some protection from the weather, yet to me being in the house seemed no different from being out in the world. *If you want to sleep*, Hannah Kallenbach's voice said, *why then do you not sleep?* I walked to the window instead and stood there with my hands clenched. An icy breeze came and went along the skin of my leg as though through a tear in my pajama trousers. *What is there for me to do but go to bed?* I thought. After all, I had no job, no wife, no child to take care of. *Nothing*, said Hannah Kallenbach. *Absolutely nothing.*

All the while, the worm of cold air disappeared and reappeared on my skin, sending my hand chasing after it in some complicated kind of foreplay. Having felt with one hand along the seam of my pajama trousers, searching for a hole, I now ran my hand along the window's edge. The sea air corroded things—it had eaten away taps and wires, pipes and light fittings—so perhaps a gap somewhere was letting in cold air. The paint flaked as I touched it. *Where are you?* I said to the hole. *Where are you, if anywhere at all?* Because the window appeared to have no metal frame, merging seamlessly into the concrete around it.

But then, beneath the left-hand corner of the glass, I felt an almost indiscernible groove in the concrete, like the dink in the head of a very small screw. Was it a screw? It looked like a screwhead but it was hard to see because it was covered over with paint. *Why don't you just unscrew it and see what happens?* Hannah Kallenbach said. So I fetched a carving knife from the kitchen. The screw was stiff, so firmly sealed over with paint that it bent back the top of the knife. But beneath another knife, it gave way. It brought me great pleasure to be *doing something*, to be using my hands again, and I lifted the screw from the wall until it came out completely, leaving a dark tunnel in its wake. Through the tunnel came a jet of cool air. It occurred to me that since a screw is always attached to something, unscrewing it must be severing something from something else, but the activity was so completely engaging that I couldn't stop going over the window with my hands for more screws, and having found them (there were half a dozen or so spaced at regular intervals), unscrewing them. At the end of the row I pressed my hand against the glass, expecting it to collapse in a heap, but it didn't. It must, I thought, have been held in place by some hidden mechanism, or limescale perhaps. In the failing light the window had become a mirror in which I saw a composition of stripes: the crumpled brown stripes of my pajamas against the black stripe of the piano against the white stripe of the ceiling, from which two strips of wire protruded from the remains of a broken light fitting.

That night I felt so lonely that I couldn't sleep. I soothed myself by imagining I was a child again, at a time in one's life when sleeping alone is not yet lonely. When eventually I drifted off I dreamt of Hannah Kallenbach's yellow room again. But this time when I opened the door at the far end of the corridor, the room I arrived in was not the yellow room but the bedroom I'd slept in as a child, only the things inside it weren't my childhood things but adult things, official-looking papers and books, ceramic pots, a pair of thick-soled sandals. Whereas the other dreams had been vignettes—at least it seemed that way to me, since I remembered only fragments—this particular dream stuck in my mind because it was long and exquisitely detailed. I was sitting on the bed in this room that was either the yellow room or my childhood bedroom or both, when someone knocked on the door. As the door opened I made out the face of Hannah Kallenbach. She stood for a moment, silhouetted in the crack of the doorway. She looked nice, standing there. In the subdued dream light her wrinkles softened. Then she smiled at me with genuine pleasure and said, *What are you doing?* and all at once, from behind her, water came rushing in, swirling around her feet in little eddies. *What have you done?* she was saying now, her voice louder. I saw that she was wearing a coat and some kind of hat. *I'm sorry*, I said. *I'm sorry.* Because I remembered that I'd been running a bath upstairs but once the tap had been opened I couldn't get it shut. Hannah Kallenbach was walking toward me with eyes narrowed and her arms crossed so hard over her chest that her breasts were flat. I didn't know what was going to happen but whatever it was aroused a feeling in me that wasn't sexual exactly, but since it was everywhere in my body, I felt it there, too. When she reached the bed, Hannah Kallenbach leaned down and pulled me toward her. *What are you doing?* I said. And she said, *I love you*. But I knew I was dreaming. So I said, *I don't believe you. Tell me again in the morning.*

VII

Whatever you love most dearly

We'd been warned of high winds and now they arrived, starting with a coordinated movement of leaves in the trees and a slapping of branches on the windows. The wind flew through the house, blowing curtains, rattling door handles, skewing pictures, causing the telephone—which hadn't rung for weeks—to tremble in its cradle. It pushed at the living-room window, which shook and shuddered and then, with one great gust, came out completely.

Blow, blow, blow, said Hannah Kallenbach, whose voice had become the dark background of my days. Avoiding the broken glass, I crossed the room. The empty window made me feel vulnerable in a way that was not entirely unpleasant. How can I explain it? Through it the tall Gothic spires of the church in the bay looked more exotic somehow. The absence of glass produced a sort of heightened receptivity in me. It made me more susceptible to the world, letting me receive its imprint directly onto myself, like a photographic negative. Through the glassless window, the purple sunrise with its disheveled horizon seemed grander, and more powerful. Everything was exactly the same as it always had been, of course it was, but there was something vague about the way my eyes registered the world. Whereas previously I could see things clearly—the trees, even their individual leaves—now when I looked out the low-flying gulls were almost indistinguishable from the white specks that came off the tops of the waves. Things were on the cusp of not being themselves. I had the idea that it wasn't my vision deteriorating but the very glue which held the objects of the world together growing old and weak.

When the wind picked up, it moved things, and when it withdrew, everything went still. It blurred the distinction between what was alive and what was not *dead* exactly, but ... well, between what had life and what didn't. That was the problem. Or rather, what enlivens things? Does it come from inside or outside? The wind blew thoughts into my head: wild, inappropriate, dreamlike thoughts. When my eyes landed on the row of agapanthus under the house, the plants gazing up at me with their big heads from the flower bed looked animate. I didn't see plants staring up at me but sentient beings whose tall stalks, depending on their uprightness or the angle of their heads, had a certain humanness. And although I knew that it was sad to attribute to flowers a character they didn't possess, that it was sad to find an animus in plants when all a plant is capable of is processing light, I couldn't help feeling that the tall flower nodding on its stalk was strong yet somehow benevolent, while the skew bloom beside it rising from its leafy body had an affect that was at once quizzical and superior.

Next door, the builders had arrived and were moving around the site tidying things, motioning for each other to come and see this or that bit of damage. Tarpaulins and sheets of chipboard were scattered around the site, not messily so much as in the positions that things might adopt over time to make themselves more comfortable. The tower itself, which by now was well underway, seemed undamaged by the various weathers. The gas lines, which men with picks and shovels had laid the previous week, were intact. So, too, were the sewers and the foundations. Only the mesh fence between the house and site had collapsed, a fence post ripped right out of the ground with earth still clinging to its foundations. Touw, who'd arrived in his usual orange handyman trousers, was standing at the fallen-down fence with one foot resting on the fence post.

I went around the living room righting pictures and sweeping up the glass and dead leaves that had blown in through the window. Several heavy-bodied spiders had relocated themselves from the garden into the corners of the ceiling. *What a mess!* I said to myself as I went around tidying things. *What a mess.* The dirt around me raised a wave of disgust so powerful that no sooner had I finished the living room than I started on the kitchen, emptying the fridge and washing the forgotten cups of tea which had been piled up in the sink since Mim left. *What a mess, what a mess.* I scrubbed the counter with steel wool until the yellow grime had come away from the grouting and the tiles had returned to their original clinical gray-green.

I made my way down the ramp to rake up the leaves and branches that had blown down from the mountain. But in the entrance hall I stopped and looked back toward the laundry. Halfway down the corridor was the washbasin. *To wash off the outside world*, the South African academic had told me. And at first I'd liked that, the idea of cleansing oneself of the outside world. After all, wasn't that what I'd come for? To be *cleansed* of something?

But this was the first time I'd actually used it and I scrubbed myself thoroughly, almost angrily, feeling it necessary to really clean myself. *What are you doing?* said Hannah Kallenbach. *I'm cleaning out*, I said. But *cleaning out* wasn't right. *Cleaning out* was how South Africans described a certain kind of burglary. Someone has been *cleaned out*, they'd say, when the burglars had taken absolutely everything. I was *flushing out*, then.

Past the washbasin, at the end of the corridor, the door was closed. I'd avoided the laundry since Mim left. It was a lonely room, such a lonely room that just the idea of it was hateful. But that morning something felt different. I made my way past the basin, down the corridor, and, having opened the door, stood for a while in the doorway with my heart beating so hard it lifted the fabric of my pajama shirt. It was a bright day but down there the air was thick, a damp gray haze. Unlike the first floor, which was raised off the ground on pillars, the rear section of the ground floor had been excavated from the rock behind it—scooped out of the mountain, you might say—which made it cave-like, especially now, when its window was almost completely covered over with ivy. The light was gone and in the dim light—it was half or almost completely dark—it was hard to make out the dimensions of the room, or where the walls met the ceiling.

Mim's things were scattered around the room. Beside the door were shoes, at least ten pairs. *What a mess*, I thought, staring into the mustiness. Flakes of paint or dust covered every surface. The floor was piled so high with things that the only way to traverse it was by walking on top of them; each time I lowered my foot it raised a cloud of dust. A shrine of sweet wrappers was piled up on a stack of magazines beside a wineglass full of cigarette ends. Mim's raincoat lay on the floor where she'd left it, having long forgotten her shape. Its pocket contained a few coins of too little value to bother with. *What a mess*, I was thinking, but there was something sinister about the arrangement of things across the room, something more than just mess, something unified, as though the objects had not just been strewn around randomly but were shying away from something. *Like the debris from a fallout*, said Hannah Kallenbach. *Yes*, I thought. But when I opened my mouth to say it—*Like the debris from a fallout, exactly!*—it felt like a heavy weight had been dropped onto my sternum and my voice came out squashed and childish. Which was apposite, I suppose, because there *was* a childishness about what I was doing, as if by tidying the room I could return things to how they were, which is of course the worst kind of wish, the wish to reverse something, the wish to say, *I take it back*, or, *I preferred it before.*

On Mim's desk—a concrete slab that must have been designed as an ironing table—was her laptop, its red light flashing in resistance to the room's gloom. When I touched it a half-finished game of solitaire appeared, causing several of the mosquitoes which invaded the house nightly (drawn to its glass windows as to a large lantern) to appear from the shadows, their affections transferred to the bright light of the screen. Beside the computer was a piece of paper. *My dearest Max* was written at the top of the page. *My dearest Max*, it said, nothing else. One side of Mim's note was rough, as if torn from a book. On the other side was a block of printed text, a section of which had been circled in blue ink: *Walls shouldn't be strong, they should be soft and enclosing.*

Then the computer went dead and the room went dark. Groping around among Mim's papers and empty sweet wrappers I found a box of matches. The lit match cast a flickering glow, illuminating a spider suspended directly above me: it was thick and velvety and didn't scurry. I took the flame to the bottom of the web and let it creep up to the spider sitting there, and burn it. For some reason—perhaps the flame had punctured a small hole in its abdomen before melting it completely—the spider began to squeal before disintegrating onto me (and Hannah Kallenbach, too, because she was also there).

I rifled through Mim's things looking for the rest of the letter, or other drafts of it. A stack of open books lay beside the computer, facedown, as though Mim had stopped reading them halfway through. *Perhaps she was bored of them*, Hannah Kallenbach said. Or the opposite. I imagined Mim in a flurry of ambition, impatient with how long it took to get through a single book, thinking, *Right! I'm going to read them all right now, at the same time.* In the pale light from the corridor, I opened the uppermost book. It was called *The Hidden Messages in Water* and suggested that the shape of water was determined by its relationship to the people around it. There were photographs of water crystals, which, if you looked at them closely, revealed minute differentiations: a glass of water which had been shouted at, said the author, appeared murky under a microscope, while one subjected to declarations of love ran clear. Beneath it was a book called *Aqueous Architecture*, which was not, as I'd expected, about buildings with sea views or water features (like Frank Lloyd Wright's Fallingwater, which has a river running through it) but about how water changed the structure of consciousness. If *The Hidden Messages in Water* believed that human consciousness changed the structure of water, then *Aqueous Architecture* believed the reverse. The author wasn't interested in buildings *made with* water, it turned out, so much as buildings *made like* water. He listed the various forms water could take: there was water, of course, but also water vapor and cloud formations. *What is a cloud?* he asked. *What would it be like to live in a fog or a mist?*

But I was paying less attention to the contents of the books than scanning their margins for traces of Mim. Here and there she had struck out a sentence in blue ink or encircled a passage or inserted a question mark or note into the margins. On one dog-eared page she'd underlined the phrase *buildings should close around a body the way a mother holds a baby*. On another, beside the words *people should enter their houses like a drop of blood entering a puddle of water*, she'd drawn an exclamation mark. I tried, by triangulating the marking to the words it referred to, to decode what she'd been thinking while she was reading, but the circles and exclamation marks meant nothing to me. I tried to gauge by the marks her pen had made what mood the hand making them had been in (a heavy underlining suggesting anger, a messy circle indicating frustration and a desire to move on). But really her marginalia were illegible, less like words or symbols than a long blue thread which had come unraveled somewhere inside Mim, and I, now, was trying to reel back in.

At first the laundry had smelled of damp walls but beneath the musty odor I began to detect a second smell, a secretive smell, hidden beneath or rather *within* the first one, because although she'd been gone for some time, Mim's perfume had been preserved in the airless room, only mixed in with the earthy scent of the walls, it'd grown deeper and muskier, more pungent, and so intensely evoked Mim's presence that all at once it made me want to weep. So I sat down and cried, or tried to, because the tears were like grout; I only managed to squeeze a few out with great effort.

Then I came across a memory. It wasn't a distant memory, nor one I'd forgotten. In fact, it was something I'd have thought of often had I not made a strenuous effort to avoid it. The memory was of the afternoon Mim had arrived in South Africa. We were driving away from the airport and I remember that as we passed the large supermarket on the motorway out of Cape Town she turned to me, glassy-eyed, and said, *You know, I really love that child* (she was talking about her sister's newborn son). She said, *I love him in spite of all the reservations I have about children. Maybe it's because I was there just after he was born* (she arrived four or five hours afterward), *but last night when I said goodbye to him it felt like it was my own child I was leaving. I felt so close to him that it seemed there was no boundary between us, particularly physically, that there was no limit to my affection for him. I mean, of course there's a limit, but . . .* For some reason we were both crying. *What are we crying about?* I said and she laughed a humorless laugh that said, *Life is funny, isn't it?*

Somewhere a dog started barking, causing another dog to bark somewhere else. On and on they went. Continuing my spring clean—which now was just a euphemism for scouring the room for clues about Mim—I came to a small metal filing cabinet. One by one I emptied the drawers, finding receipts, bank statements, a list of ingredients (*polenta chili anchovy mint*) for a meal I don't remember eating, expensive cuff links, a silk scarf, French toothpaste, a prescription for medication I didn't recognize, a variety of circulars addressed to *Whomever it concerns*, a picture of me as a boy with a severe side parting, a racetrack packet of contraceptive pills (half of which had been popped from their plastic sockets), a stopped watch, a number of spiders the size of Ping-Pong balls, and a letter to Jan Kallenbach from someone who didn't know that he was dead so they couldn't reach him.

The bottom drawer was locked so I knelt down on the floor and forced it open. Inside was a small notebook with a black cover. I hesitated before removing it, then did, but left the room without opening it. *What are you waiting for?* Hannah Kallenbach asked me, and I said, *I don't know.* It wasn't the contents of the notebook which frightened me, it was its secretiveness. It must, I thought, have contained the something I didn't want to know, or why would she have kept it in a locked drawer where I wouldn't find it? All evening I carried Mim's notebook around but did nothing with it. At the end of the day, I filled up the blue mosaic bathtub and sat in it, not washing myself, just sitting there with the notebook on my sternum, studying the weeds insinuating themselves through the edges of the skylight. Then, putting it aside, I slid down beneath the surface of the water until my head and shoulders were covered and the sea, from underwater, sounded like a distant volcano.

VIII

The only way to understand the sea is to drop a grid on it

For days I delayed opening the notebook through a series of deferrals. I'd pick it up while brushing my teeth then put it down again so as not to ruin the experience by reading in the bright light of the bathroom. I'd pick it up while waiting for the kettle to boil then put it down again so the squealing wouldn't break the flow of my concentration. I'd bathe for hours and comb my hair in various ways. The more I waited the more afraid I became of the notebook, and the more afraid I became the more I kept it closed, as if by doing so its contents might remain imperceptible or even disappear. But the more I carried it around the heavier it became, until the experience of carrying it had become so embedded in me that it was hard to tell whether it was its weight I was carrying around or mine. At the end of each day I'd lie on the chaise, angle the reading light down, pick up the notebook to read it, then put it down again because, having held the notebook so constantly, my wrist ached.

Each day and into the next, it rained. Through the window the sea swelled and the boats looked small. Grasses slid down the mountain with so much earth attached to their roots that it seemed the mountain itself was disintegrating. There was something primitive about the rain. It made me want to *see* people or *be with* people. It wasn't a calming rain, making uniform watery noises, it was a whipping rain that beat on the skylight and came in sideways through the glassless window. The newspaper showed flooded streets and floating cars. The story of the weather had become the story of the defenses people constructed against it. The radio spoke about stocking cupboards with tins. Cartoon characters converted household items into flotation devices (the legs of the dining-room table are removed to become oars, the flat tabletop is a raft).

One day, as the afternoon neared its ending, with a vegetable soup on the stove and the potatoes far from cooked, I went to the living room to read. I shut the door, sat down, covered myself with a blanket, picked up the notebook and might very well have put it down again when, because the binding was weak, a clump of pages fell out. The outermost page was a blank white expanse with no words for my thoughts or feelings to snag on, and I let my eyes wander up and down it as if at a strip of magnificent coastline.

Overleaf were a few lines of Mim's messy scrawl. *Brace yourself,* said Hannah Kallenbach. What was I afraid of? A letter, perhaps. *Dearest Max*, the letter might read, *if you are reading this then I must be dead.*

But the notebook didn't contain notes about Mim, it contained notes about the sea. They weren't written in full sentences but were phrases stacked up on top of each other like a poem. *The sea is infinite, the sea is eternal*, et cetera, nothing insightful, just the usual generalized observations people make about the sea. I turned the page and found more banal observations. *So this is it*, I thought. *I can see why she hid this away. These are just the nonsense clichés people have been making about the sea for centuries.*

I thought about the kind of people who come to the sea to look at it, how they put themselves down on whatever rock or bench is around and gaze for hours into the distance as though something out there makes life seem meaningful, or at least less incomprehensible. *What are they looking at?* I asked myself. *What do they see when they see the sea?* Most people seemed to find the sea deeply interesting but it held no particular depth or virtue for me. The most profound effect the sea had on me was that sometimes, from the living-room window, it quite literally made me want to throw up. I'd always thought that people who liked the sea were people who didn't like society, that it was people who'd failed in their relationships who turned to the sea. There was something in their glazed faces—leaning on harbor railings, walking along the crumbling promenade, staring over the tops of their newspapers—which disturbed me. It seemed they wanted to be immersed in it, that as they looked out at the sea they entered into a special relationship with it which, to a certain extent, entitled them to speak to it. Because people who spent too much time looking at the sea did start to commune with it, as if nature held the answer to all of life's important questions, their expressions suggesting that they were not so much watching the sea as conversing with it. I could tell from the way they sat, dead still, that the sea *spoke* to them and that they, for their part, were receptive to its communication. But what was the sea saying to them? The sea didn't speak to me. *What do you say to them that you won't say to me?* I asked the sea, but the sea was silent and had no communication to make.

The sea glints, Mim had written. *The sea seethes.* In this vein were written an extraordinary number of pages. *The sea is lonely* and *The sea is wide* and

The sea looks like the ridges on the palate of a person's mouth. The sea sighs, she wrote, though it seemed to me that what the sea was really saying, if anything at all, was *why* or *who* or *whywhywhy*. It was apparent from the number of pages Mim had written, mottled with traces of her rubbings-out—*The sea shivers*, she'd written, no, *quivers*, no, *shakes*—that she'd watched the sea closely, methodically even, yet as the notebook progressed her notes said less and less about anything, everything just ended up as some metaphor to do with water. Sometimes, despite being neither forensic nor lively enough to be worth repeating, an observation would appear twice—that the sea was like *sequins*, for instance, or *the metallic blue of the BMWs they used to use in road-trip movies*—which was disconcerting, breaking, as it did, the promise inherent in reading, that, line by line, as one thing leads to another, one is all the time *going somewhere*, that if one keeps going, one will eventually *get somewhere*, to some end or conclusion.

As the day wore on it became harder to read, not because I didn't like what I read but because the clouds were dark and it was too dim to read without squinting. An image of Mim floated into my mind, clarifying for a second before it was swallowed up again. Sometimes I'd come into the laundry and find her sitting at the desk, her face whitened by the light from the computer screen. *What are you doing?* I'd ask, and she'd say, *Nothing*, though I could see from the reflection in the window behind her that she was playing solitaire. *What did she see when she looked at the sea?* I wondered. *Perhaps it was just something to look at*, said Hannah Kallenbach, *a convenient place to rest her eyes*. But why did she need to put it into words? It occurred to me that this business of writing things down must have mattered to Mim personally, that in among her thoughts about the sea must be other thoughts; that someone who fixed their eyes for hours and hours on something a thousand miles from nowhere must find, after a while, that it was their own thoughts they came up against. But the more I read the less I understood, since as the notebook progressed, perhaps because her hand was tired, Mim's handwriting loosened and the words began to lean away from me, as if hiding something. *What are you looking at?* they seemed to say. *We're just words! We don't like being scrutinized in this way!*

The point about the sea, it seemed, was not to look at it but to capture it somehow, to turn it into words the way a painter might fix the sea in variegated shades of blue or a composer might transcribe it into waveform music.

So I went to the window to see for myself. The ocean looked exactly as I had expected it to look: vast and blue and boundless. *What are you doing?* asked Hannah Kallenbach, though being in my head she must have understood without my having to explain. I scoured its surface for signs of life but apart from the odd seagull there was nothing to be found. I tracked the minute tide movements, trying to decipher the order underlying the fleeting patterns on its surface, which were always changing depending on where you focused your eyes. I opened the notebook and recorded my observations. *Parts of it are clear*, I wrote, *others are scummy. It moves from the pavement to the horizon, then back again. Some things get sucked beneath the surface while others stay floating on top of it.* Then, because I didn't know what I was doing, I closed the notebook. *You want to see something*, said Hannah Kallenbach. *You want the sea to show you something and when it doesn't you think it's wasting your time.* So it was that my first attempt to study the sea came to nothing.

Later, because I tried a second and third time, the experience was almost traumatic. My many vague thoughts masked one very clear one: there was simply too much of it. Just the idea of it filled my mind with inconceivably large numbers. In fact, I felt a strong temptation *not* to look at the sea, though I fixed my eyes on it anyway, as if by staring hard enough they might dip down a thousand yards and get to the bottom of whatever mystery lay beneath the gulls and dead leaves. But however hard I tried, I couldn't see what you're meant to see when you look at the sea. So, having dedicated myself for some time to observing the water, I came to the conclusion that nothing I could say about it was insightful.

The rain stopped and I went up to the solarium. The sun came out from behind the clouds (*the sun came out from behind the clouds*, we say, though really it's the clouds that are passing) but the paving had been sunk in water so long that it had lost its hardness and gone soft and almost wood-like. A crab scuttled out from under a flowerpot and darted away. I watched a municipal worker clearing leaves from the railway tracks, jumping back each time a train squeaked past. Fishermen bent over their hooks and tackle, so accustomed to the sea that they paid it no attention. Whereas from the living room the close-up view of the sea made it seem restless and constantly moving; from the solarium, seen in its entirety, it was obvious it wasn't going anywhere. *The sea twitches*, I thought. *Perhaps that's why she watched it, without worrying, not even for an instant, about waking to find it gone from the bay.* I zoomed out, letting my eyes relax until the sea beneath me was just a long blue line which, at a certain point, became the horizon. Nothing stood out. Nothing drew itself to my attention. In fact, the more I looked at the sea, the less I seemed to see it, and this special way of *not looking* produced a feeling in me that I was sort of there and sort of not there, a feeling which lasted for a few minutes until, because it troubled me, I wrote it down—*There are times*, I wrote, *when I'm looking at the sea and it's all so dull I can hardly be sure I even exist*—and felt myself again. *I stand here thinking these strange philosophical thoughts*, I wrote, and felt a sort of happiness come over me, or comfort maybe, as if there were suddenly two of us, as if my writing down my thoughts was a way of keeping myself company.

After half an hour or thereabouts the rain returned, a reprieve doubly cruel for its brevity, since there was neither enough time for the puddles to be reabsorbed into clouds nor for the sun to blast away all my thoughts. When I came downstairs, the phone was ringing. In all the months of living alone, I'd not gotten used to being alone. When the phone rang I couldn't help hoping—just for a second while the caller's identity was still unknown—that it was Mim calling, knowing at the same time that the moment I picked it up the disappointment would make my stomach drop as it does coming over a steep hill. When I picked up the phone, the line was quiet. *Hello?* It was a woman's voice which eventually spoke. *Hello?* it said again because, perhaps since I'd not spoken to anyone for a long time, I'd forgotten to say something. Hannah Kallenbach's voice was warm and soft but loud at the same time, as though amplified by its surroundings, like when someone is calling from a phone box. *Are you okay?* she said. *I just wanted to find out how you were... How you are, I mean.* The question gave me a strained feeling: like happiness, or sadness, or both (as if we've two different names for the same feeling), or maybe something else entirely which just shares their intensity. *Oh*, I said, *thank you.* Her voice lowered, taking on the kind of conspiratorial tone that suggests one is about to be let in on a secret. *I was worried that the phones were down*, she said, *so I wouldn't be able to reach you.*

The moment I put the phone down I lost all memory of the conversation. With it went the memory of everything that had happened around it, all of which disappeared the way that, when you wake up, you lose dreams. I tried to orient myself with questions like *What day is it?* or *What was I saying five minutes ago?* or *Who was it I was talking to on the telephone?* but couldn't answer any of my questions so I stopped the test and tried to forget it, too. My mind was blank apart from the word *Hannah*, which circled in my head like a trapped insect. *Hannah*. Like *Mim*, it read the same in both directions. *Hannah, Hannah*. I said it twice, as if to expel it by saying it out loud, then a third time because it was a pleasant sound, enveloping, with no harsh plosives for the tongue to trip over.

That night, although I knew I was alone, I didn't feel that I was alone. When I walked to and fro in the windowless room, the darkness turned the glass wall into a mirror so it looked like there were two of us walking in the room at the same time, the other following me like a double. And when I looked out at the invisible black sea, the lighthouse consoled me by casting its beam across the water, illuminating some gulls floating in the darkness. And later, when it was quiet and the restaurant music no longer echoed through the bay, the sea sound was like someone breathing in the room with me. I lay down and closed my eyes, feeling a clenching in my heart. Shaking my head from side to side, as if to refuse something, or to burrow my way into sleep, I caught myself muttering, *Everything will be okay, everything will be okay in the end*, without knowing why, as if somewhere inside, I knew that being asleep was more dangerous than being awake.

IX

The sun came out from behind the clouds, we say,
though really it's the clouds that are passing

Morning arrived and I opened my eyes, pushing the notebook slowly to one side. It wasn't light yet. I could measure the distance of things by their color: those nearest were bright and vibrant; those furthest away were gray, as if covered in ash. *It must be Sunday*, I thought, because the building site was quiet. As my eyes adjusted to the dark, I saw Hannah Kallenbach leaning against the radiator, looking down on me with her special piercing gaze. *What are you looking at?* I said. And she said, *I like watching you wake up. I like the way that, for a few moments, you're okay*. Because for a few moments everything was calm and then it began to shake. I thought there might have been an earth tremor or that a washing machine somewhere was on spin cycle, but the glass of water beside my bed had no ripples on its surface. For a moment

(since each night in dreams I reversed Mim's leaving so that in the morning it happened all over again), I had the notion that the bed was moving because Mim was beside me, sobbing maybe, or masturbating. Then I heard the sounds of something dropping, and again the house shook as a crane off-loaded a stack of bricks from a van parked on the street into a large metal skip. I couldn't see the crane in its entirety, all I could see was the apex of its bent elbow as it lifted the bricks, swiveled, and released them with a loud crash.

Gradually, the tower had begun to resolve itself into a form I could recognize. On top of the square podium the skeleton of the building had been erected—a dozen or so round floor plates supported by thin columns. There were no outer walls or windows yet, just these evenly spaced floor plates rising up around the large columns for the lift shafts, with staircases zigzagging between them. I could see the stairwells and the corridors, and the rooms leading off them. The electrics had gone in and bits of wiring poked from where the plug sockets and light switches would be. Touw had arrived on-site in a pair of maroon britches and leaned a tall ladder against the wall of the apartment tower. He was fitting a bright green flag onto a flagpole made from a piece of timber. TOUW STUDIO said the flag. MAKING EXTRAORDINARY PROJECTS HAPPEN! The builders, watching as he tightened the rope of the flag around the makeshift flagpole and, turning his hands, fastened it, looked to be experiencing collective bemusement.

All the while, it rained. The sea was flinging up brown sand and lifeguards had raised red flags to keep surfers off the huge waves coming in, each one beginning almost before the previous one was over. In the months since I'd arrived, the building site had been animated by changing noises. In the early days, while the builders were breaking ground, I'd mostly heard loud drilling and jackhammers breaking up rocks. Then had come the peaceful time while the foundations were being laid, which in due course had given way to the construction stage, with contractors arriving on site each morning, each with a different job, making a different sound. Mostly there were delicate sounds—the fine metal sounds of a chain swinging, its links clashing in a metal chord; the even roar of an electric sanding machine—accompanied by the large, generous rumble of a concrete mixer. But sometimes, since I couldn't always see which instrument or tool each sound corresponded to, I had to imagine a machine producing a tired squeal or one which emitted tapping sounds in such a quick rhythm that—in the same way as the multiple notes of a saw's teeth sounding close together are identified simply as "sawing" or the many incisions of a drill are just called "drilling"—they merged into a single high-pitched whine. So that during the day, as I lay on the chaise, my thoughts were constantly being infiltrated by odd hypotheses. When, for instance, I heard stones knocking together, I pictured stones being cleaned in a large washing machine, and when I heard a metallic scratching sound, I pictured somebody sweeping the dirt with a metal-bristled broom, and when a faint whirring filled the air, I imagined that someone somewhere was grinding coffee or sharpening a pencil with an old electric pencil sharpener.

What disturbed me, however, was not the mysteriousness of the individual sounds—which, in themselves, were not especially aggravating—but the sounds that the builders (more of whom arrived every day) made working simultaneously. Because although I knew that each of the builders was acting independently, oblivious of the others, I couldn't help searching for some kind of synchronicity between them, as though, like an orchestra tuning up before a performance, their many tools were just warming up for the moment, always imminent, when they would come together into some kind of coherent organization. My ears, unable to switch off this hope for the resolution the site seemed to be crying out for, were constantly alert for any regularity, believing always that a hammer striking (*one, two, three*—pause—*one, two, three*) might be counting the rest of the instruments into rhythm, or that some sonic coincidence, like the scrape of a spade running for a few seconds in parallel to the grating of a drill, signified something *more*. As though the bricklayer smoothing mortar and the roofer laying flashing and the plumber installing a pipe and the workman transferring gravel from something into something else were, all the time, on the verge of aligning themselves, of synchronizing into some form which would reveal the underlying structure according to which the site was arranged.

All day, I listened to the completely unpredictable orchestration of banging with a burning sensation in my chest. The lack of rhythm drove me nearly insane and I couldn't wait for six o'clock when the mechanical sounds gave way to the human sounds of laughing and talking as the builders packed up and went into the corrugated hut to change clothes. But the moment the gate closed and its chain clinked shut, I regretted their departure since my ears, having listened with such attentiveness during the day, couldn't switch off their sensitivity to every sound. Even when the world went quiet, they heard the smallest noise acutely. Especially at night. No sooner had I closed my eyes than my highly attuned ears would detect some sound—the creaking of a ventilator or my foot rubbing against the bed linen—which, like a conductor raising his hand, would draw in some other sounds, and then a whole host of sounds which during the day would have meant nothing to me, but in the dark, when it was hard to link the noise to the object it came from, seemed strange and sinister. However calm I felt when I lay down, within moments of switching off the light, my ear would fixate, for instance, on what sounded like two pieces of wood being knocked together, a sound which seemed so threatening that I'd stay dead still for minutes—hours, even—hardly breathing in case the air squeaking through my blocked sinuses alerted the intruder of my presence. Then the noise stopped. Then it started up again, only this time it seemed less like two pieces of wood knocking together than a thin piece of wood creaking, like a wooden clotheshorse being folded away. For a moment I felt relieved—*it was just someone folding laundry*. But of course it couldn't be a clotheshorse because why would an intruder be folding a clotheshorse, and in any case, I didn't have a clotheshorse, I hung the washing over a cable strung between two trees. It was as though the inner membrane of my ear had been worn away. Sometimes I even took the sound of my own breathing for the sound of an intruder's footsteps dragging their way along the corridor toward me. And at those times, above all, I missed Mim. I longed to be able to turn over and know by her unchanged breathing or the calm expression on her sleeping face that whatever rustling or scraping had frightened me didn't worry her, so there was nothing for me to worry about either. *What are you so afraid of?* I'd comfort myself, trying not to respond to every noise that came out of the dark with a paranoid start. *There's nothing to worry about.* But when, in the middle of the night, a sound emerged from the darkness, it was so alarming that I'd jump out of bed, convinced that I was not alone—*those are definitely footsteps!*—and rush to the window only to fasten my eyes onto complete blackness. For a moment I would hear something, a scratching for instance, as though somebody—an archaeologist?—were chiseling away at the mountain, and I'd say, *Hello?*, then, suddenly timid, *Hello?* again, picturing whomever was out there staring back up at me.

Even when I fell asleep my ears, like two sentries guarding me overnight, stayed open. So it would happen sometimes that long after midnight, in the time of deepest sleep, I would wake because someone was calling for me, or not calling *for* me so much as calling out my name with a rising inflection, the way someone hearing a noise when they think they are alone calls out *Hello?* I'd try to ignore the sound—it wasn't Mim, I told myself, *of course not*—and although I knew it was just a dream, I couldn't help believing that it *might be* her, that she *might be* downstairs, standing at the door calling for me, waiting for my reply. Despite myself, I'd lie there, making not the slightest movement, in case she called again, sometimes even responding with my own *Hello?* and lifting my head from the pillow in the hope that something other than the ticking of my watch could be heard on the other side of the room. Then I'd fall asleep again, but too soon, before the dream had been fully blown away by wakefulness, so that sometimes Mim's presence remained and I'd wake again during the night to feel her prodding my shoulder. *I must be snoring*, I'd think, rolling over, but her hand would keep up its prodding until I opened my eyes and found a dark shape standing over me. *What are you doing?* I'd say, and when she didn't reply, I'd try to shush myself back to sleep—*Ssh*, I'd say, *Ssh, ssh, you're dreaming, it's just a dream*—but nothing my eyes told me as they grew accustomed to the dark erased the feeling of dread in my heart.

It rained for days, for weeks, each daily outpouring coming more voluminously from the clouds than the last. The rain had breached the boundaries of the house. It came in through the glassless window of the living room and through the corners of the ceiling where the flat roof was improperly sealed. Damp rose on the walls of the entrance hall where the foundations were too shallowly laid and filtered into the upstairs walls where water had penetrated the facade. The roof had become a breeding ground for mosquitoes. Clouds of them drifted into the living room, where the atmosphere was better for living. They surrounded me so that it felt like I was being tried by a council of mosquitoes—*What is he waiting for?* they said. *He must be waiting for something, something in particular.*

Before long, the tea-colored stains began to leak and I arranged a number of saucepans under the ceiling so there were now a variety of places around the house which produced a regular rhythm as heavy raindrops fell into the metal pots. The dripping sound had the opposite effect to the unpredictable orchestration of the building site. Where the noises from outside were so irregular that I was constantly being alerted to their presence, the water falling into the pots, tempered as it was by the many layers of roofing and ceiling materials, was so evenly distributed that it had a reliable beat and my mind soon grew accustomed to its presence. The enduringly uniform tempo of the rain dripping into the house provided me with a sense of security. Hearing it, like a baby soothed by a ticking clock, I felt reassured, both of the rhythm's own constancy and of the house's ability to protect me. Since the rhythm, which stood in counterpoint to the chaos outside and the vagaries of the rain (which raged against the skylight, settling into a beat for a moment or two only before the wind changed direction and it became unfamiliar again), distinguished inside from out, giving the impression, so seldom experienced anymore in the house, that *being inside* meant *being separate from the outside world,* so the experience of the rain, from inside, was detached: I could sit there and watch it like a film about rain.

For days the urge to play the piano had found outlet in a constant foot-tapping and teeth-chattering and pressing of fingers against thighs. Now I sat down at the piano. Chopin's preludes fell open, out of habit, on the "Raindrop" prelude. The ivory keys were brown around the edges and the fingering penciled into the score had faded but my hands remembered where to go, the right hand carrying in the melody, the left coming down repeatedly on the A-flat which runs throughout the piece. My hands were cold—a luminous, bloodless yellow—and however hard I tried, my left wrist kept collapsing. *The little bird!* I'd remind myself, because my Russian piano teacher had told me to keep my wrist high up as though cradling a bird's egg beneath the palm of my hand, but it was no good, the muscles had atrophied since the accident and didn't have the strength to hold it for very long.

The "Raindrop" prelude's recurring A-flat, I had always thought, was one of piano playing's greatest paradoxes. The fact that technically it was so easy—with its many repeated notes—made the prelude seem generally more straightforward than, say, pieces with lots of complex finger maneuverings. Yet its simplicity was precisely what made it so complicated, because how can a person strike a single note over and over at exactly the same volume and tempo? After all, apart from the physical challenge, since a finger strains when performing the same movement repeatedly, the pianist's problem is to find a way to play the note *with feeling* so that the repetitiveness of a single note heard again and again with absolutely no variation does not become boring.

As is traditional among pianists, I had always alternated between the index and third finger to keep the tempo regular and stop either from becoming overtired. But the scar tissue from the accident, or perhaps the metalwork itself, had stiffened my fingers so the index finger of my left hand came down heavily and loudly on the A-flat with a regularity so exact it was almost militant. And whereas previously the left hand had intuitively responded to the melody in the right, making subtle adjustments in volume and tempo and tone to add color, softening instinctively in the places where the melody was pleading or seductive and vulnerable, now it came down on the A-flat with absolute consistency.

That my left hand had acquired this mechanical quality ought to have neutralized the prelude's capacity for misery but instead it brought it to the fore. And as I played automatically, like some kind of pianola, my mind thought about other things, thoughts unrelated to the music, thoughts about Mim, for instance, and my childhood piano lessons. I remembered the two grand pianos my Russian piano teacher had kept side by side in her converted garage, a black Yamaha for everyday playing and a Steinway for special occasions and Shostakovich, and how if I arrived early I stood outside to listen to the breathy *puh-puh-puh* of her keeping time. Sometimes, if I stood on my toes to reach my eyes over the glass, I'd see her leaning forward, her pockmarked face elongated and sheared in two by the swirled brown windowpane, so that her long dark hair bled into the piano as though she was not so much playing it as being sucked in by it.

What do you like so much about this piece? said Hannah Kallenbach. Because although the fingers of my left hand felt detached, like a set of nerves which had come apart from the rest of the nervous system, my eyes had closed and I'd tilted over the piano as you do when you're about to fall over. *I can't explain it*, I said. It wasn't the narrative of Chopin's illness or the rain that moved me, it was the way my hands moved in relation to each other. They seemed to understand something about the piece that I had never understood myself. Before, they had been a pair, operating together, but now they were independent. Previously, in the opening bars, my left hand, responding to the right hand's tentative melody, had softened and slightly slowed its repeated A-flat to echo it, but now, with its pins and fused joints, it ignored it and just kept on striking its key as firmly and evenly as a pulse. And a few bars on, as the rain swelled and the melody became dejected, whereas previously the left hand had elongated its A-flat in sympathy with the melody, now its note remained unswayed. That night, as I sat at the piano, the piece wasn't just a retelling of the story of Chopin and his situation (like mine, only more lonely), it was something that was happening, there on the piano, a relationship unfolding between two hands which were like two characters, one expressive, the other unexcitable, who'd been together once but were now detached.

Because the left hand refused to accompany the right, the right hand missed its partner. I could tell by the way it played, moving its fingers faster and more expressively, that it was using one flirtatious technique after another to try to be reunited with it. At first the right hand played delicately, pressing its fingertips timidly on the keys as if it were something fragile or naive, something that needed taking care of. Then, because the left hand wasn't moved, its rhythm and volume remaining consistent, the right switched tactics: instead of courting the left's sympathy (or protection, maybe), it feigned indifference, as if attempting to arouse the left's interest through its own lack of it. And when the left hand resisted, the right expressed its unhappiness by playing more gently and delaying the resolution of its leaps of melody to make them sing with special sweetness. In the absence of feeling from the left, the right hand strained its cadences until they seemed so ... so ... *How can I explain it?* Well, they seemed so full of feeling. The more the right hand failed to get a response, the more desperate it became. Alone, it played faster, with an almost hysterical speed. Until the climax, when the storm is at its most vicious, where it suddenly became heavy, giving the impression—because it had slowed so much that it was out of sync with the rhythm—of disorientation, as if it were dazed or unable to manage without assistance. And as the right hand's fingers climbed the keyboard, drifting away from the left hand, expanding the melodic theme, slowly, by a note or two—tentatively at first, then with resolve—the strain of the gap became apparent and, worried it had gone too far, the right hand returned to the original melody and tempo (though the high notes lingered in the air, since the sea air had corroded the hammers and deprived the piano of the warmth for which Bechsteins are known). For some time it went on like this, the right hand extending the melody a little further, for a little longer, prolonging the distance between itself and its old companion until, reaching the cadenza, when Chopin fears Sand dead, it held its high note for such a long time that my heart—worrying that, like a kite that nobody is holding, the melody would not come back down—sped up and I felt certain my left hand would finally *do something*, that it would swell up from beneath the melody and *catch it*. But it didn't. Obedient to the score, it remained restrained, firm, steady, even-tempered, so resistant to being carried away that it might have seemed cruel had it not at the same time felt somehow comforting, as if the absence of sentiment was not a way for the left hand to distance itself from the right but the opposite, a way to contain it.

Michael Hofmann

THE CASE FOR BREXIT

I dropped my new shoes in the stream, thinking perhaps
They would get there before me, like two drowned Jews
Trundling along the seabed to Jerusalem. My immigrant parents lost patience
    and thrashed me.
The best thing that ever happened to me was on the boat.
I've no idea what it was. Then Tilbury. Or Harwich. Or Southampton.

I got eggshells crushed with lemon juice for the calcium and its better
    absorption.
I got buttered bread with a little bitter chocolate grated over it.
I got glabrous soured milk with cinnamon and sugar.
I got kohlrabi and celeriac and other nonexistent vegetables,
Like so many chimeras and hippogriffs.

I got *Kinderkaffee* from malted barley, and *Katarzynki* from Mr. Continental,
    but only on Thursdays.
I got vermilion worm medicine, with bitter lemon
That didn't begin to take away the color or the taste.
The four of us round the table. We all had to do it. It was like a suicide pact.
It was the winter of '63, the Plath winter. I barked for months.

I juggle the numbers, the way I sang my times tables
On the swing. (They are all I have in the world.) The sevens, the nines.
They mostly begin with the scalene 19– . I swing them around, sling them
    and swing them.
Lennon and Kennedy and Punk and the Wall and the Moon.
Big numbers, jagged numbers, like someone with very heavy weights.

I invented sepia. Sepia came for me. Something discolored
Behind me, in my past, like a hobbled Clovis ad. Our charlady smelled so
    terrible,

My father smoked a pipe ("Fair Play") after she was gone. My young mother
    still giggled.
She and my father played badminton on the street at night.
You could read the *Times* past eleven. (You could read the *Times*.)

School uniforms, playground fights. Goalposts. Polar ghosts. British bulldogs.
I should have liked to be called Roger or Arthur. The bully Brian Lorry
    pummeled and pummeled.
All Trutex or Aertex. Caps. Striped ties and the striped elastic belt with the
    snake-mouth hook.
Melrose, RHS, Loretto, George Watson's, Boys' *and* Girls'—all mauled us.
I was at bat for days without scoring a run.

Practically everything was a shibboleth. Harwich was a trick.
Berwick was a trick. Worcester was a trick. Geoffrey was a trick. I didn't
    know Sundays were no-go.
My home German was compared to a serendipitous knowledge of Welsh;
I knew better: it was less. My only friend, McVicar, had a Greek mother.
    Maybe Clytemnestra.
They moved further North, so that he could be with Prince Charles.

Somehow

———

DANIELLE DUTTON

omehow, they were swimming in the canals.
Later this part seemed hazy, but somehow
they were all there: Lila, her little boy,
and James, a former student. Whether James had
arrived with Lila and her son or was simply also
there enjoying the day is unclear, but at some point
it became clear that they were there together.

It was a popular place to swim, so close to the
city, with shops and cheap bars on the wharf above.
Lila was conscious of having on her shabbiest swim-
suit: flesh colored, a one piece. It had lost its elas-
ticity yet was strangely smaller than when she had
bought it. Her breasts were barely covered by the
fabric, but this did not seem to her remotely sexy.
She kept checking to make sure her nipples were
not exposed. It was like wearing a swimsuit made
of plastic wrap, everything pressed down and on
display. Impossible to say what James was thinking.
She was not tuned in to his thoughts. He was only

there, somehow, in a way he'd not been before. Her son was a fine swimmer. Little eel. His little-boy skin glistening in the light. He laughed and laughed, and James laughed with him. She watched them from a distance. A seagull floated past. She'd started her period that morning and wondered if when she got out of the water the crotch of her suit would be red. Her breasts felt huge, misshapen even. James looked over and smiled.

A few weeks earlier, before the semester ended, Lila had gone to hear a famous Buddhist give a talk. The lecture was in the city but at a Buddhist center situated in a large and wild-seeming park, large enough and wild enough, anyway, that when she got to its center, where the wood-and-glass lecture hall stood, it seemed she'd somehow managed to get outside the city. The air felt cool. She stopped in some shade beside a clump of purple flowers. Forest bathing, she thought. Had she heard that on a podcast? Inside the hall the famous Buddhist cleared his throat. He began by telling a story about Laurie Anderson going to hear a different famous Buddhist give a talk in a different city, where apparently she pledged to be kind for the rest of her life. Lila had just been reading that Laurie Anderson was NASA's first-ever artist in residence. She'd imagined NASA launching Laurie Anderson into outer space. It turned out she'd just visited some labs. In a simulator in a lab in California, she wrote in her red notebook, There will one day be a staircase up to Mars. Certain of the researchers were unimpressed. "What's she going to do, write a poem?" one said. Anyway, the story went that after she pledged to be kind for the rest of her life, Laurie Anderson freaked out. Unsure whether she was upset because she'd promised too little or because she'd promised too much, she approached one of the Tibetan monks and asked him out for coffee. The monk said yes and sat down to the first espresso of his life. He sipped and listened, and then he began to talk, faster than he'd ever talked before, saying, essentially, Knock it off. He said the mind is like a wild white horse. Or he said *her* mind was like a wild white horse. Lila wasn't sure—the woman beside her was coughing horribly. Was Laurie Anderson's mind like a wild white horse, or was everyone's? Was her mind— was Lila's—a wild white horse, too?

When it was time to go, James asked for a ride. They tossed wet towels and shoes into the trunk of her car. Lila's boy was four. On the drive, he told them he was a dog. He'd been a dog all along, he said, ever since he was born. "You're a funny guy," said James. "I'm not a funny guy, I'm a dog," he said.

James laughed. His teeth were very white. "Where should I drop you?" Lila asked. The hairs on her arms were stiff from the salt in the canals. But James said he could easily walk from her place. He'd been to her apartment before, she remembered, with several other students after a lecture downtown. The speaker was a Bosnian writer who described his poems as torsos without heads. It had snowed and she'd given them coffee. Now it was summer and the city was steaming. She'd thrown on a pair of denim shorts over her ill-fitting suit.

At the door to her apartment, Lila offered James water—what else was there to do? He stood in the kitchen as she went to rinse her son and put him down for a nap before returning to the bathroom to rinse the salt off herself. The apartment was spare: a kitchen, a bathroom, her son's room painted blue. No vacancy, she thought, peeling off her suit. Of course there was another room, her own, down the hall, where she stood in two towels, one around her body, one around her hair, when James came in and took off his clothes and laid down on the bed. Almost instantly she thought of an essay by Eileen Myles. It was an essay about a painter named George whose former student comes into the room, takes off his clothes, and lies down on the bed. It's quiet in the room, but thousands of sounds rush around outside. George paints the former student. Fucks him, too? A "luminous back," she remembers reading. He paints from memory. But can you pull the noise of the world apart and say *that's* a cicada, *that's* a plane, *that's* two men kissing upstairs? And then there was that dream about a different former student, a graduate student in geology who wrote a poem about erosion. "There are no perfect circles in geology," it began. In the dream, he followed her to a modular hotel, pushed her against a door, and she fucked him through the night. And is it in the same essay that Myles admits seeing the Taj Mahal in person is a total disappointment? I paint, George says, because I like to paint. In one painting a woman serves a man a bowl of soup. Between his fingers are fingers, between his thighs her hand. Between his lips she sees his teeth as white as paper and remembers the famous Buddhist calling a sheet of paper the sun. A piece of paper is a cloud. It is the rain and the logger and the logger's mother, too. And if you look hard enough, you'll see yourself on the page—tits heavy, fingers spread, waiting for something to happen. Isn't that what she'd written? Isn't that what he'd meant? Wait, stop. That was a different one. That was a different one. That was a whole other essay.

VEDA

CONTRIBUTORS

PETER COLE's most recent book is *Hymns & Qualms: New and Selected Poems and Translations*.

KATHLEEN COLLINS (1942–88) was a writer, filmmaker, and civil rights activist. *Notes from a Black Woman's Diary: Selected Works of Kathleen Collins* is forthcoming in December.

RACHEL CUSK's novel *Kudos* will be published in June.

MÓNICA DE LA TORRE is the author, most recently, of *The Happy End/All Welcome*. She teaches in the Literary Arts Program at Brown University.

DANIELLE DUTTON's most recent book is the novel *Margaret the First*. She is cofounder and editor of the feminist press Dorothy, a publishing project.

PATRICIO FERRARI was born in Argentina and currently lives in New York. He has translated Fernando Pessoa, António Osório, and Laynie Browne.

FORREST GANDER is a poet, translator, novelist, and playwright. His new collection of poetry, *Be With*, is forthcoming in August.

CARY GOLDSTEIN is vice president, executive director of publicity, and senior editor at Simon & Schuster, and an advisory editor of *The Paris Review*.

KYLE HENDERSON is an illustrator and architect in London.

MICHAEL HOFMANN's translation of Alfred Döblin's *Berlin Alexanderplatz* has just been published. His new book of poems, *One Lark, One Horse*, will be out later this year.

ISHION HUTCHINSON is the author, most recently, of the poetry collection *House of Lords and Commons*.

MAJOR JACKSON is the Richard A. Dennis Green and Gold Professor of English at the University of Vermont. His latest volume of poetry is *Roll Deep*.

KATHARINE KILALEA is the author of the poetry collection *One Eye'd Leigh*. *OK, Mr. Field* is her first novel.

STEPHEN KURTZ is a writer living in Mexico City. His fiction has appeared in the *Kenyon Review*, *Salmagundi*, and *Partisan Review*.

NICK LAIRD's most recent novel is *Modern Gods*. His new collection of poems, *Feel Free*, will be published in the summer.

DOROTHEA LASKY is the author of *Milk*. She teaches poetry at Columbia University School of the Arts.

CHIA-CHIA LIN's first novel is forthcoming in 2019.

ANGE MLINKO's most recent collection of poems is *Distant Mandate*.

JOANNA NOVAK is the author of *I Must Have You*, a novel, and *Noirmania*, a book of poetry. She is a founding editor of *Tammy*, a journal and press.

ALEJANDRA PIZARNIK (1936–72) was one of the most significant contributors to twentieth-century Argentine poetry. A collection of her French poems, *The Galloping Hour*, will be published in July.

NICOLE RUDICK is the interim editor of *The Paris Review*.

JOY WILLIAMS's most recent book is *Ninety-Nine Stories of God*. She is the recipient of *The Paris Review*'s 2018 Hadada Award.

TERRY WINTERS's recent drawings, accompanied by Peter Cole's poems, will be published in *Terry Winters: Facts and Fictions*, in conjunction with the exhibition of the same name, which opens at the Drawing Center, New York, in April.

IMAGE CREDITS

Cover: Art © Etel Adnan. Hand lettering by June Glasson. Page 59: Getty Images/ Pedro Pardo. Pages 64, 70–71 (top), 76–77, 84–87: © Etel Adnan, Courtesy Galerie Lelong & Co. Pages 67–69, 72–73, 78–79: Courtesy the artist & Sfeir-Semler Gallery, Hamburg/Beirut. Pages 71 (bottom), 74–75: © Etel Adnan, Courtesy Galerie Claude Lemand, Paris. Pages 80–81: © Etel Adnan, Courtesy Galerie Lelong & Co. Paris. Pages 82–83: Courtesy Callicoon Fine Arts, New York. Page 137: © Zorn B. Taylor.

wine of passion grace & spirit
www.seresin.co.nz

READINGS

92Y CHRISTOPHER LIGHTFOOT WALKER READING SERIES

Mon, Mar 19
PETER COLE AND
LAURA KASISCHKE

Thu, Mar 22
YOKO TAWADA AND
TATYANA TOLSTAYA

Thu, Mar 29
AMINATTA FORNA AND
ALAN HOLLINGHURST

Mon, Apr 9
ELIZABETH STROUT
AND
JOHN EDGAR WIDEMAN

Thu, Apr 12
**JEREMY IRONS READS
T. S. ELIOT'S "FOUR
QUARTETS"**

Thu, Apr 19
LESLIE JAMISON AND
GREGORY PARDLO

Mon, Apr 23
JULIAN BARNES AND
LORRIE MOORE

Thu, Apr 26
THE TENTH MUSE WITH
EILEEN MYLES

Mon, Apr 30
**TRACY K. SMITH,
JENNY XIE** AND **JAVIER
ZAMORA**

Wed, May 2
ADAM ZAGAJEWSKI AND
DUNYA MIKHAIL

Thu, May 3
CURTIS SITTENFELD
AND **MEG WOLITZER**

Thu, May 17
STEPHEN GREENBLATT

Wed, Jun 6
ROXANE GAY AND
TAYARI JONES

BOOKS & BAGELS

Sun, Apr 8, 11 am
KAREN KUKIL AND
PETER K. STEINBERG
on Sylvia Plath's Letters

Sun, Apr 22, 11 am
DEVONEY LOOSER
on Jane Austen

Irons

Smith

Gay

AND THAT'S NOT ALL!
VISIT **92Y.ORG/POETRY** TO SEE THE
FULL LINEUP AND PURCHASE TICKETS

92Y 92nd Street Y | Unterberg Poetry Center
Lexington Avenue at 92nd Street, NYC 4, 5, 6

The Plimpton Circle is a remarkable group of individuals and organizations whose contributions of $2,500 or more help advance the work of The Paris Review Foundation. The Foundation gratefully acknowledges:

1919 Investment Counsel • David M. Adler • Aēsop • Alfred A. Knopf • Theresa Gavin & Mark Almeida • Peggy & Keith Anderson • The Anna-Maria & Stephen Kellen Foundation • Jeff Antebi • Gale Arnold • R. Scott Asen • Debbie & Mark Attanasio • Amanda Urban & Ken Auletta • Ijeoma A. Azodo • Jessica Yager & Robert P. Baird • André Balazs • Kyra Tirana Barry • Mahnaz Ispahani Bartos & Adam Bartos • Alexandra Styron & Edward Beason • In Recognition of A. William J. Becker III • Helen & William Beekman • Charlotte Beers • Mr. & Mrs. Alexandre Behring • Jessica Marshall & Peter N. Belhumeur • Robert Bell • Amy Bennett • Liz & Rod Berens • Kathryn & David Berg • Desiree Welsing & Olivier Berggruen • Joan Bingham • Blaine & Tim Birchby • The Blackstone Group • Leslie Tcheyan & Monty Blanchard • Carol Rosetto & John Blondel • Bloomberg Philanthropies • Suzanne Deal Booth • Susanna & Livio Borghese • Winthrop Brown • Timothy Browne • Brunswick Group • Sarah Burnes • John Burton • Ariadne & Mario Calvo-Platero • Camilla Campbell • Lisa & David Carnoy • Lisa & Dick Cashin • Allan Chapin • Sarah Teale & Gordon W. Chaplin • The Chittenden Fund • Michael Chon • Ronald C. Christian • City National Bank • Susanna Porter & Jamie Clark • Nancy & Fred Cline • Stacy & Eric Cochran • Daniel Cohen • Caryn & Rodney Cohen • Bernard F. Conners • Wendy Mackenzie & Alexander Cortesi • Georgia Cool & Christopher Cox • R. Boykin Curry IV • Michel David-Weill • David Zwirner Books • Jerome Davis • Charlotte & Michael de Anda • Raymond Debbane • Debevoise & Plimpton LLP • Deborah DeCotis • Gayatri Devi • Diane von Furstenberg & Barry Diller • Eva Dillon • Linda Donn • Douglas Wright Architects • Jane C. Dudley • East Rock Capital • Janet Ecker • Kelly & Randolph Post Eddy III • Gwen Edelman • Inger McCabe Elliott & Osborn Elliott • Emerson Collective • Rachel Cobb & Morgan Entrekin • Jeffrey Eugenides • Sandi & Andrew Farkas • Farrar, Straus & Giroux • Clara Bingham & Joseph Finnerty III • Rachel Davidson & Mark Fisch • Jeanne Donovan Fisher • Estate of Richard B. Fisher • Todd Fisher • Gary Fisketjon • Michelle Flint • Judith & David Foster • Martha Kramer & Neal J. Fox • Brandon Fradd • Wendy Stein & Bart Friedman • Arlene Hogan Fuller • Minnie Mortimer & Stephen Gaghan • Mala Gaonkar • Martin Garbus • Toni K. & James C. Goodale • Maria & Noah Gottdiener • Francine du Plessix Gray • Grayson Family Foundation • Sol Greenbaum • Michael Greenberg • Tracy Day & Brian Greene • Mark Leavenworth Griggs • Grove Atlantic, Inc. • Grubman Shire & Meiselas, P.C. • Lucy & Lawrence H. Guffey • HBO • Christina Lewis Halpern & Dan Halpern • Ms. Julia W. Haney & Mr. William M. Haney • Denise & Tom Harnly • Harper's Magazine • Alexes Hazen • Gabriela & Austin Hearst • Margaret & William Hearst III • Alexander Hecker • Drue Heinz • Kathryn & John Heminway • Jody & Emil Henry • Hilaria & Alec Baldwin Foundation • Ken Hirsh • Christopher Hockett • Olivia & Warren Hoge • Julie Iovine & Alan Hruska • Sean Eldridge & Chris Hughes • Elizabeth Hunnewell • Susannah Hunnewell • ICM Partners • Vicki Iovine • Valerie Stivers & Ivan Isakov • Frederick Iseman • Ala & Ralph Isham • Kathleen Begala & Yves-André Istel / Y. A. Istel Foundation • Kenneth M. Jacobs • Amy & John Jacobsson • Joele Frank, Wilkinson Brimmer Katcher • A. Robert Johnson • Karine Chen Foundation • Mary Maxwell & David Keller • Katheryn C. Patterson & Thomas L. Kempner, Jr. • Lisa Atkin & Tony Kiser • Nina Köprülü • Steve Kossak • Mariana Cook & Hans Kraus • Alan Kriegel • Phineas Lambert • Duff & John Lambros • Fabienne & Michael Lamont • Mr. & Mrs. Steven Langman • Sherry Lansing • Evie & David Lasry • Blair Brown & Dwight Lee • Jenny Lee • Bokara Legendre • Susana & Pierre Leval • Anne Kerr Kennedy & Matthew G. L'Heureux • Barbara & Robert Liberman • Wendy Gimbel & Doug Liebhafsky • Vera Szombathelyi & Gary Lippman • Hilary Mills Loomis & Robert Loomis • Josephine & William Lowe • Peter Lusk • Thomas Lynch • Renee Khatami & John R. MacArthur • Macmillan & Holtzbrinck Publishers • Laurie & Mitchell Major • Alexandra & Terrence Malick • Shelby & Anthony E. Malkin • Ellen Chesler & Matt Mallow • Marianne

Boesky Gallery • Mark & Amy Tercek Foundation • Mr. & Mrs. Donald Marron • Tatiana Maxwell • Ellen & Frank McCourt • Jeanne McCulloch • Joanie McDonell • Stacey Hadash & Terry McDonell • Anne Hearst & Jay McInerney • McKinsey & Company • Keith & Jon Meacham • Sandy Gotham Meehan • Maria Semple & George Meyer • Michael Werner Gallery • Lorrie Moore • Alexander B. Miller • Tara Gallagher & Luke Mitchell • Charlotte Morgan • Shelley Wanger & David Mortimer • Walter Mosley • Anju & Deepak Narula • National Endowment for the Arts • Arvid Nelson • Bruce S. Nelson • Lynn Nesbit • Mr. & Mrs. Arthur Newbold • The New Yorker • Francesca & Richard Nye • Marsha O'Bannon • Euelyn J. Offenbach • Abdim M. Okanovic • Wendy Flanagan & Christopher O'Malley • Lynn & Harry O'Mealia • Linda Ong • Open Road Integrated Media • Neil Ortenberg • Other Press • Erin Overbey • Eunice & Jay Panetta • Paul Kasmin Gallery • Park Pictures • Elena & Michael Patterson • Paulson & Company • Radhika Jones & Max Petersen • Joan Ganz Cooney & Peter G. Peterson • Elise Pettus • Marnie S. Pillsbury • Sarah Dudley Plimpton • Ted Porter • Annie & Edward Pressman • Denise & Jonathan Rabinowitz • Henry Ramos • Random House • Red Mountain Fund • Regele Builders, Inc. • Manuel Reis • Esther B. Fein & David Remnick • Betsy von Furstenberg Reynolds • Mary Fulham & James Reynolds • Richard Roth Foundation • Valerie Riftkin • Matthew Roberts • Sage Mehta & Michael Robinson • Roxana Robinson • Mr. Bruno Roger • Emmanuel Roman • Lauri Romanzi • Joanna & Dan Rose • Marjorie and Jeffrey A. Rosen • Mr. & Mrs. Benjamin Rosen • Mary Lee Stein & Mark Rosenman • Mr. & Mrs. William Rosoff • Robert de Rothschild • Marc Rowan • Perri Peltz & Eric Ruttenberg • David Salle • Frode Saugestad • Amy Atkins & Forrest Sawyer • Schlosstein-Hartley Family Foundation • Irene & Bernard Schwartz • Stephen A. Schwarzman • Andrea Schulz • Akash Shah • Vivian Bower & Lawrence Shainberg • Georgia Shreve • Stanley & Sydney Shuman • Alan Siegel • Jake Siewert • Robert B. Silvers • Mona Simpson • Skadden, Arps, Slate, Meagher & Flom LLP • Samuel A. Skeen • Gibbs M. Smith • Maurice Sonnenberg • Jill Spalding • Ashley Baker & Davin Staats • Jean Stein • Joan & Michael Steinberg • Antoinette Delruelle & Joshua Steiner • Rose Styron • Allison & Stephen Sullens • Sullivan & Cromwell LLP • Nan & Gay Talese • Thendara Foundation • Marcia & Mark Thomas • Melissa Thomas • Tibor de Nagy Gallery • Tierra Innovation • Bardyl & Anne Bell Tirana • Joseph Tomkiewicz • Maggie & Amor Towles • Catherine & Wolfgang Traber • Traphagen Family Foundation • Elizabeth Trundle • Cecelia Peck & Daniel Voll • Kira von Eichel • W. W. Norton & Company • Wachtell, Lipton, Rosen & Katz • Liza & Paul Wachter • Amanda & John Waldron • Alison Merritt Weaver • Rosemary Fine Weaver • Mercedes Martinez & Chris Weitz • Leslie Marshall & William Weld • Wenner Media • Tom Werner • Judith Cox & Benjamin C. Weston • Donna & Walter Wick • The William & Mary Greve Foundation • William Morris Endeavor Entertainment • Bunny & Bruce Williams • Susan Rushing & Jim Windolf • Hope Brock Winthrop • Victoire Bourgois & Lucas Wittman • Stuart Woods • The Wylie Agency • Dylan Yaeger • Aroldo Zevi • Amy Zilliax • Marlene Hess & James D. Zirin

The Paris Review is grateful for the support of its friends. Please send your tax-deductible contribution to The Paris Review Foundation, 544 West 27th Street, Third Floor, New York, NY 10001. Contact Julia Berick at 212.343.1333 or jberick@theparisreview.org.

Past Publishers Sadruddin Aga Khan, Bernard F. Conners, Ron Dante, Deborah Pease, Drue Heinz, Antonio Weiss

Editors Emeriti Maxine Groffsky, Donald Hall

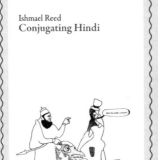

Is the dream gone?
Malleable, lucid thoughts,
Imagine our emotions - obsolete,
A future - bright,
Futuristically, urban,
Urbanized by the child,
Childhood - ephemeral,
Also obsolete, sweet cocoa,
Look at the skyline rising amongst the skies,
through and through,
Admire the movements,
And try to remember - the child in me.

CASA BOSQUES ——
CHOCOLATES

www.   casabosques.co
x   vvstudio.net

HAMMER

Stories
of
Almost
Everyone

January 28–May 6, 2018

HAMMER MUSEUM | Los Angeles | Free Admission | hammer.ucla.edu

PARTNERS

We Proudly Congratulate

JOY
WILLIAMS

Recipient of the

2018 HADADA AWARD